I0827442

SHALL HE FIND FAITH ON THE EARTH?

Shall He Find FAITH on the Earth?

A CRITICAL ACCOUNT OF THE CRISIS IN THE CHURCH

ABBÉ CLAUDE BARTHE
Translated by David J. Critchley

Angelico Press

Originally published in French as *Trouvera-t-Il encore la Foi sur la terre? Crise de l'Église, histoire et questions*

First published in the USA
by Angelico Press 2026

For information, address:
Angelico Press, Ltd.
169 Monitor St.
Brooklyn, NY 11222
www.angelicopress.com

Ppr 979-8-89280-177-5
Cloth 979-8-89280-178-2
Ebook 979-8-89280-179-9

Book and cover design
by Michael Schrauzer

When the Son of man comes,
will he find faith on the earth?
—Luke 18:8

CONTENTS

TRANSLATOR'S NOTE

Translations of papal documents are taken where possible from the Vatican web site, or are made direct from the French of Abbé Barthe. Extracts from other works have been translated direct from the French of Abbé Barthe. The extracts from the schema *De Ecclesia* (chapters 6 and 9) have been freshly translated from the Latin. Translations of the traditional Mass are taken from the bilingual missal of Abbot Cabrol, 13th edition, Tours, 1950; translations of the French versions of the conciliar Mass are made directly from the French as quoted by Abbé Barthe, and will often differ from the corresponding authorized English translations.

The footnotes are the work of the translator. They give brief explanations of French historical details mentioned by the author, or sources for quotations and other references in the text, with details of English translations where possible.

INTRODUCTION
Vatican II, the Rupture

DID THE REFORM of Vatican II reverse the reform of Pope Gregory VII? The case can be argued, insofar as Vatican II rejected the status that the Church had claimed in full since Gregory's time, when the papacy had asserted as never before the principle of the freedom of the Church. As the Spouse of Christ, she understood herself to be on earth the supernatural totality of Christ's Mystical Body. When she confronted the great sixteenth-century rupture of the Protestant reforms, she set in motion an immense effort comprising the Council of Trent and the subsequent Counter-Reformation leading to a doctrinal, spiritual, and liturgical consolidation of what had been transmitted. Following the French Revolution, Catholicism continued throughout the nineteenth and twentieth centuries to assert the freedom of the Church (the *libertas ecclesiae*) in the face of states of a new type, which refused in principle to acknowledge her freedom. Catholicism tried to halt the wave of liberalism, a much more radical wave than Protestantism, even though it came from the same individualist source. The effort was not cost-free. In reality, the very vigorous anti-modernist campaign of the papal Magisterium (comprising Pius IX's encyclical *Quanta Cura* of December 8, 1864, condemning modernism,[1] the accompanying *Syllabus of Errors*, and Pius XI's encyclical of December 11, 1925, *Quas Primas* on the Social Kingship of Christ), weakened as it often was, one must admit, by the diplomatic policy of

[1] Modernism may be summarized as the belief that the Catholic Church should come to terms with contemporary developments in secular thought.

Ralliement,[2] seemed more and more to be a voice crying in the wilderness.

Vatican II, in the four years from 1962 to 1965, overturned this edifice by putting forward a certain number of "intuitions" (religious freedom, ecumenism, the principles of inter-religious dialogue) in which the Church recognized that outside the Spouse of Christ there were supernatural entities, though admittedly incomplete; paths to salvation, though deficient; and a communion with Christ, though imperfect. The result was that the Church now claimed for herself no more than the right shared in contemporary human society by all spiritual associations, for all of whom she requested from the regulatory state, ideally a liberal democracy, the same religious freedom. This was the polar opposite of what she had asserted as the freedom of the Church, and magisterial texts such as *Quas Primas* became unreadable. The shock was considerable, and all the more so because the "opening to the world" of the Church took place at the same time as a surge in the process of secularization, a surge which was itself substantially aided by the developments in the Church. Out of all the political, spiritual, and disciplinary consequences that followed, the most striking was the collapse of mission, the Church's very *raison d'être*, seen in the thinning out of the principal workers of the harvest, priests and religious, and in the reduced numbers of converts and of practicing Catholics.

Weakened by her fight against the world brought to birth by the French Revolution, the Church, still strong and well-resourced, notably in people, used what remained of her prestige, concentrated in the person of the pope, to abdicate from her royal status, an abdication symbolized by Paul VI laying aside his tiara. What

[2] *Ralliement* was the papal policy which, instead of maintaining the Church's outright opposition to the republican regime, urged Catholics to support the more moderate French republicans with a view to obtaining concessions for the Church.

the Church's leaders overturned was what was left of the authority which the popes had inherited from the Fourth Lateran Council, from the Council of Trent, and from the *Syllabus*, or in other words, what was left of a Tridentine and anti-modern Christian ecclesiology.

Vatican II, however, is now part of history, like any event from long ago. It took place in the first half of the 1960s, in a period quite different from our own, the period of Kennedy's America and of the consumer boom of the *Trente Glorieuses*.[3] Since then, the world in which Catholics live has changed greatly, notably because of this self-effacement of the Church. Today's world is only interested in Catholicism insofar as the world requires Catholicism to give up its final symbolic opposition to hyper-modernity. We are faced with the paradox that this modernizing council, because of its antique clerical make-up, appears today to be out-of-date, almost medieval, in the midst of a world to whose formation it nevertheless made a powerful contribution. Catholicism, however, still dominates the stage, not least because of the unshakeable opposition which it continues to excite and which obliges its defenders to engage in static, positional warfare.

In the context of this cold war, Catholicism has, with the texts and passages that most perfectly express the thought of the Council, put forward in practical terms a liberal Catholicism which can be characterized as wanting to bring the Church and her beliefs into line with the modern world, with the intention, always frustrated, that the world would make a space for the Catholic religion and grant it a hearing. This conciliar version of liberal Catholicism has the distinctive characteristic, in comparison with its predecessors (the nineteenth-century liberal Catholics, the minority at the First Vatican Council, the Americanists, the modernists), that it has been

[3] In France, the "thirty glorious years," 1945–75, marked an exceptional period of economic achievement.

driven forward by a party which took control of doctrinal authority at the Council. For that reason—because modernity was imposed by anti-modern organs of government—the opposition was largely powerless.

For all that, it very quickly became clear that the Council had not succeeded in winning unanimous support for its project: the opposition *within* the Council, given strength by the liturgical issue, became a traditionalist opposition *to* the Council and demonstrated that it could not be overcome. This opposition drew additional strength from an entire reformist or "restorationist" world, which fundamentally, and whatever it said, never really fully accepted Vatican II. The unity of what remained of Catholicism was thus broken and—we will return to the point at the end of the work—every attempt to repair or conceal this split has so far failed.

We have to insist on it. When the Council is judged against the Church's foremost objective, that of mission, the verdict is that it was fundamentally a failure. Not only does the Church no longer win converts, but the number of her faithful, her religious, and her priests is shrinking to the point where she seems on the road to extinction, at any rate in the West. Even if we suppose that the hemorrhage was caused not by Vatican II but by the societal revolution of 1968—a supposition that the chronology and the evidence do not support—the Council completely failed to staunch the flow. When Vatican II opened, Catholicism was certainly already sickening, but the cure which the Council applied greatly aggravated the disease. So much so that, even though the Council's entire object was to adapt the message to its contemporaries' sensibilities and to attract them to a rejuvenated, transformed, and above all modernized Church, it failed even to catch their interest.

The means by which this change was effected, a change which failed finally to transform the image of the Church, consisted in weakening two things. It diminished the rigor of the message—"I am the way, and the truth, and the life" (Jn 14:6)—now considered to be such that no one would listen to it. It also undermined the authority of those passing on the message—"He who hears you ['you' being the pope and the bishops] hears me ['me' being Christ]" (Lk 10:16)—considered to be insupportable in today's world. We have moved from a robust set of beliefs, proclaimed by the one Church and Ark of Salvation, to an altogether more fluid teaching, given by a Church content to be thought of as just one of society's spiritual components. This is not to suggest that the Council's decrees were the ultimate cause of the unprecedented crisis which has afflicted the Church ever since, but without a doubt they set it in motion and revealed its extent.

To put it brutally, Vatican II was a council that abdicated its responsibilities.[4] To be as precise as possible, we could say that it wrapped a new method of teaching, the "pastoral" approach, around the Church's traditional dogmatic function. Vatican II, as we have been told a thousand times, was not a council like the others. It said itself that it was atypical, as much in its basic purpose as in its authority, with content and authority being the two poles of the magisterial function in the Church. The content of this teaching is the transmission of the deposit of the faith, not by repeating it in the same terms as those in which it was originally expressed, but in the form of a new illumination, taking account of the attacks that it is undergoing or the failures in understanding that it suffers (for example, in matters of Christology, the new illumination provided by the Councils of Constantinople, Ephesus, and Chalcedon, relative to the initial dogmatic position worked out by the Council of Nicaea). So far as the Church's authority is concerned, it is that of the pope or of the pope and the bishops together: he or they make use of their full responsibility as the successor of

---

[4] French, *un concile de démission*. It seems impossible to express the sense in English that is equally concise.

Peter and the successors of the apostles to require, in the name of Christ, the unconditional adherence of the faithful to what they teach as being part of the deposit of faith. There can be no transmission of the faith without the faithful being required to believe whatever is stated by the terms in which this deposit is transmitted.

From the work of the ecumenical councils, from the midst of the reforms on which agreement has been reached, from the legislative pronouncements, and sometimes from the decrees of union with separated churches, we therefore retain as essential and specific the doctrinal definitions provided by these solemn assemblies. In reality, the assembly of the pastors of the Church is first and foremost the clearest means of expressing the Church's living Magisterium, or more generally of its living Tradition, to the extent that it is the living exposition of the deposit contained in Scripture and in the Tradition that makes up the faith. Ever since Nicaea, whenever the pastors of the world unite, they have done so first of all to make audible the voice of the Good Shepherd proclaiming the truth which the hearer must believe if he is to be saved, and then also to set down the Church's rules of conduct and to stimulate its mission, always in tandem with the transmission of the deposit.

Now Vatican II, in essence as well as in form, chose a different option. In its doctrinal work, we can observe that a decisive role was played by three texts which contribute no new illumination, but mark a real innovation in comparison with the body of previous teaching. These texts arose, as we shall see, from a unique ecumenical project worked out by the Secretariat for Christian Unity, which led to three separate texts: the decree *Unitatis Redintegratio* of November 21, 1964, on ecumenism; the declaration *Nostra Aetate* of October 28, 1965, on relations between the Church and non-Christian religions; and the declaration *Dignitatis Humanae* of December 7, 1965, on religious freedom.

Ecumenism, in the wider sense of a recognition that the diversity of religious beliefs has a certain legitimacy, is therefore the kernel of the novelty that the Council wished to introduce, from the doctrinal point of view. So far as concerns the difference between progress through new illumination and progress by innovation, there is the well-known response of Saint Vincent of Lérins to the question, "So can there be no doctrinal progress in the Christian Church?" "Certainly," replied Saint Vincent, "there must be progress, and a great deal of progress… but with this proviso, that this progress is real progress for the faith and is not a change: the essential characteristic of progress being that a thing grows while retaining its identity, while the characteristic of change is that a thing is transformed into something else."[5] Now there is certainly a change in the affirmation that there is an "imperfect communion" or a communion which is "not full" between the Church and non-Catholic Christians, or in other words that separated Christians are not really cut off from communion with the Catholic Church, but are incomplete Catholics.[6]

"Imperfect communion": this teaching, which was deliberately neither black nor white, lacked—and for good reason—ultimate authority. The decision had been taken that the Council would only be "pastoral," that is to say that it would have no dogmatic authority, a decision inspired perhaps by the "priority of the pastoral" elaborated by Father Yves Congar in *Vraie et fausse réforme dans l'Église*, about which we will talk later. The principle that Vatican II was an atypical council, asserted many times following the Council, was first enunciated in John XXIII's famous inaugural address: the Second Vatican Council, he said, unlike all previous councils, would issue neither positive dogmatic assertions (in the

---

[5] St Vincent of Lérins, *Commonitorium*, chap. 23.

[6] Second Vatican Council, Decree *Unitatis Redintegratio*, November 21, 1964, no. 3.

form of canons) nor negative assertions (in the form of anathemas).[7]

When the Magisterium involves itself as the Magisterium, it can only do so fully. On this occasion therefore, it was only half engaged. Its entry onto this *via media*, moreover, had something like unanimous support. For the majority at the Council, this approach had the advantage of allowing a more "open" teaching, without the risk of contradicting the previous teaching. However, the minority, outflanked from the very start, was also able to turn this approach to its advantage: it quickly based its arguments on the absence of infallible authority from the texts, which it thought would deprive the texts of any absolute character.

In fact, even before we speak of an absence of authority, we could speak of an absence of clearly defined content (something which is particularly striking in the decree on ecumenism, *Unitatis Redintegratio*, which, astonishing as it may seem, contains no proper definition of ecumenism—although that is true also of the declaration on non-Christian religions, which takes care not to define what it means by religions). Whatever we make of this "fuzziness," if we admit that there is a certain legitimacy to the diversity of Christian or non-Christian faiths we imply, whether we like it or not, that God wishes (or does not condemn) religious pluralism and that God wishes (or does not condemn) a plurality of Christian confessions. That is what the *Document on Human Fraternity*, signed in Abu Dhabi by Pope Francis and the Grand Imam of Al-Azhar, states explicitly and unconcernedly: "The pluralism and the diversity of religions, colour, sex, race and language are willed by God in His wisdom, through which He created human beings."[8]

The result was that, as much in content as in manner,

---

[7] John XXIII, Address *Gaudet Mater Ecclesia*, October 11, 1962, no. 7.

[8] Francis and Ahmad Al-Tayyeb, *Document on Human Fraternity for World Peace and Living Together*, February 4, 2019.

some concessions were made to pluralism, and so to relativism,[9] as Vatican II put into practice a certain opening to the modern *Weltanschauung*, or worldview, in conformity with the mission with which John XXIII, in summoning the Council, entrusted it.

These points should certainly not eclipse the fact that the corpus of texts issuing from the Council contains some most beautiful passages, some advances, and some noteworthy points (on the foundations of the sacramental character of the episcopate, on the conditions for the exercise of the ordinary Magisterium), and some profound reflections, such as the decree *Ad Gentes* of December 7, 1965 on the missions. But it nevertheless seems that each text, taken in context and above all as part of the entire corpus of the Council's texts, forms part of the project of identifying a third way. The most "open" passages are balanced by traditional declarations. Classical declarations are accompanied by markers allowing them subsequently to be rendered harmless. Thus, "The use of the Latin tongue is to be maintained in the Latin rites, except..."[10]

If we follow the political maxim that "revolutions prevent reforms," we could note that, if we restrict ourselves to doctrinal matters, the Council, under an outward appearance of being greatly innovative, prevented the formulation of new clarifications responding to questions posed in the heart of today's world. To return to the example of ecumenism, it would have been important

---

[9] Relativism is the belief that absolute truth is non-existent or at best unobtainable, and that the only truths which can be identified are all relative to, or dependent upon, the context of their time. Applied to religion, this implies that claims such as that of the Catholic Church to be the unique teacher of the truth are only partially valid. It implies that what is true in one context may not be true in another, and it may suggest an equality between religions in that each is or may be true in its own context.

[10] Second Vatican Council, Constitution *Sacrosanctum Concilium*, December 4, 1963, no. 36.

to explain how elements of truth and salvation, often greatly mixed up, are found sociologically incorporated into entities which are not supernatural, the separated churches, and that a missionary approach to a Protestant, aimed at bringing to life the potential in his baptism, differs from a missionary approach to an atheist.

There is one massive fact that supports the analysis made so far of the non-authority of Vatican II, an analysis rendered inescapable by the undeniable authority of the ideology, in this case that of the "spirit of the Council": instead of a council that interpreted, we had a council that itself required interpretation, in very different ways. In other words, the Council never undertook the proper role of the classic Magisterium, namely the interpretation of the deposit of faith and of the Magisterium to date. In one sense, the most radical accusation that one can lay against Vatican II is the well-known statement that it must be interpreted "in continuity with tradition." Far from saving Vatican II, this reveals the Council's impotence, for the most recent council has always been the definitive expression of the interpretative tradition: it should be Vatican II interpreting tradition. The fact that it is thought incapable of doing so is the entire problem.

All other things being equal, one can say the same about the new liturgy, which no longer possesses the ritual framework corresponding to the dogmatic framework of the Church's teaching. The liturgy of Paul VI, like the Council, and for analogous reasons, itself requires interpretation. And we all know how one can multiply the different interpretations that have been made of it. The famous saying *lex orandi lex credendi*, so far as content is concerned, applies to the relations between the conciliar teaching and the liturgical reform: the transition from transcendent to immanent underlying the liturgical reform of Paul VI corresponds to the "opening to the world" of the new Magisterium. But we should note that the saying *lex orandi lex credendi* refers to the framework of liturgical law. Thus we will observe that, just as the teaching of Vatican II is not expressed in the form of a law of faith, so the development of the liturgy of Vatican II no longer corresponds to the requirements of what is properly described as a law of prayer. The almost infinite variety of possible options, the translations—or should we call them adaptations—in a multitude of languages, and the widely diverging personal interpretations of each of those who play a role, all show that the liturgy that has issued from the reform is in no sense a rule: the new liturgy is in essence non-rule. It removes rules, as do the insights of the *nouvelle théologie*.[11]

In sum, Vatican II has placed the Church in a position where there are no standards. This is a very modern position, in which non-law (essentially, here, a doctrinal non-law) plays the role of law and takes its place. It is just as if—something unheard of in the Church's history—the Magisterium as such, which distinguishes and decides definitively, either did not dare, or did not want, to engage.

---

[11] The *nouvelle théologie* is described in detail in chapter 4 below.

CHAPTER 1

The Church of the *Syllabus* and its Ambiguities

WE NEED TO return to the period which followed the rupture between society and religion, and which extends from the end of the *Ancien Régime* to the universal establishment of democracy in the final third of the twentieth century, the period of the search for a way that could not be found.

In the nineteenth century, when the rupture was still recent, one can understand that Catholics—whether liberals or the so-called intransigents—had not understood the problem in all its fullness. The liberals did not understand this rupture (or refused to understand it) in theoretical terms as corresponding to what it was in reality, namely a wish to drive the Church out of the public space. For these liberals, the Church had to integrate herself into the institutional structures which were progressively separating religion and society. She even had to speed up the separation, which was presented as eminently desirable: no more a lamp set on a stand, no more privilege in a society that had become pluralist; but merely the common right of all, just like all the other beliefs or the absence of belief. With a naïveté that is sometimes touching, the liberals thought that the new framework was an opportunity. This was the thinking of Monsignor Henri Maret, dean of the Faculty of Theology at the Sorbonne during the operation of the Concordat of July 15, 1801, and the theologian most representative of the idea that the Church should come to terms with the new principles, and of Charles de Montalembert, a flamboyant advocate of this coming to terms, who—in line with the formula of Cavour—called for "a free Church in a free State."[1] Both Maret and Montalembert, along with a strong minority of Catholics, hoped that in the new freedom Catholicism would recover an influence that, for as long as it remained tied to dreams of a restoration of a Christian world, it was losing day by day.

Opposed to them were the intransigents: ultramontanes who supported papal infallibility and were violently hostile to the ideas of the French Revolution and of nineteenth-century bourgeois society, and whose economic anti-liberalism would give birth to what would soon be called Social Catholicism.[2] Even though they did not want to compromise with the new principles, they had nevertheless in practice not understood the direction of the change that had occurred in the State. Although they developed a very acute critique of the retreat from God, they continued to call on this State, built on radically different principles, to act as if it were still sacral in nature.

That gave rise to ambiguities that were almost incapable of resolution. Thus the priest and philosopher Félicité de Lamennais, during the reign of Charles X (1824–30), controversially attacked Gallicanism and the union of throne and altar and promoted the separation of Church

---

[1] The Concordat of 1801, signed by Pius VII and Napoléon, gave formal recognition to the French Catholic Church for the first time since the Revolution. Napoléon substantially modified it in 1802 with the Seventy-Seven Organic Articles, but it lasted formally until the Law of Separation of 1905. Cavour's formula *Libera Chiesa in Libero Stato*, meaning a Church free to conduct her own affairs, while the State conducted itself on secular principles, was exemplified in the Italian Law of Guarantees of 1871.

[2] Ultramontanes supported greater papal control of national or local churches. In the seventeenth and eighteenth centuries ultramontanes had often been opposed to the claims of the Gallican Church or the Jesuit Order; but in the nineteenth century ultramontanes typically saw the papacy as the bulwark against the spread of modernism.

and State.[3] We can agree with him that monarchy in accordance with the terms of the Constitutional Charter of 1814 (a charter whose recognition of religious liberty Pius VII had already condemned in his Apostolic Letter *Post Tam Diuturnas* of April 29, 1814) was not intrinsically Christian.[4] From all points of view, the preservation of the Gallican heritage, which in accordance with the Charter partially submitted the Church to the King, was most regrettable insofar as this submission (the nomination of bishops) remained in place under the essentially liberal regimes which followed the Restoration. However, it remains true that even if Lamennais' practical analysis was correct, he was wrong in terms of the teaching of the Church—of which the pope would soon remind him—when he laid it down as a principle that the Church should accept the constitutional framework consisting in the freedom of the press, of education, of expression, and of worship. If we may adopt the later terminology created by *La Civiltà Cattolica,* the journal of the Roman Jesuits, following Montalembert's speech at the Congress of Malines in 1863, Lamennais was proposing as a thesis—that is, as a principle—something that the Church could only recognize as a hypothesis, a situation that should merely be tolerated.[5]

---

3 Félicité de Lamennais (1782–1854) was the author of *De la religion considérée dans ses rapports avec l'ordre politique*, 2 vols. (Paris: bureau du Mémorial catholique, 1825–26). Gallicanism, exemplified in the Four Gallican Articles of 1682, held that the French Church should be largely independent of the papacy, and conceded considerable control over the Church to the king.

4 The Constitutional Charter of 1814, granted by Louis XVIII following the restoration of the French monarchy, confirmed many civil liberties and remained in force until 1830.

5 For the terminology of thesis and hypothesis, see Father Carlo Maria Curci, "Il congresso cattolico di Malines e la libertà moderna," in *La Civiltà Cattolica*, October 2, 1863. A thesis, in this context, is a position which the Catholic Church maintains at all times. A hypothesis is a position the truth of which is dependent on another proposition, the truth of which is still debated. As a solution, therefore, a hypothesis is merely provisional.

Gregory XVI condemned Lamennais' views with the encyclical *Mirari Vos* of August 15, 1832, describing them as "madness" and quoting Saint Augustine, "What worse death of the soul is there than freedom for error?"[6] Gregory's successor, Pius IX, condemned Lamennais' views with even greater severity in the encyclical *Quanta Cura* of December 8, 1864, and in the accompanying *Syllabus of Errors*, the high point of papal anti-modern teaching. But Gregory XVI also confirmed the establishment by his predecessor, Pius VIII, of diplomatic relations—something which at the time equated effectively to recognition—with the July Monarchy (including treating Louis-Philippe as a "Most Christian King"), although the July Monarchy was well known to be founded on the principles condemned in the case of Lamennais.[7] What is more, Gregory XVI had just condemned the revolt of Polish Catholics against the Orthodox Czar in his encyclical *Cum Primum* of June 9, 1832—just as Pius XI would abandon the Mexican *Cristeros* ("for the sake of the Church," as Yvon Tranvouez put it) in his encyclical *Iniquis Adflictisque* of November 18, 1926—something which quite rightly could only damage Lamennais' position. The reason for Gregory's policy was that, despite being a *zelante* (intransigent) pope, he was deeply afraid of a complete loss of legitimacy. He was as it were incapable of contemplating such a situation, and so in a Europe that had been shaken by revolutions he allied himself with whatever could be seen as an "authority instituted by God."[8] And from another point of view, if he was to

---

[6] St Augustine, Letter 105.2.

[7] The July Monarchy is so named from the revolution of July 1814 which brought about the abdication of Charles X and the proclamation of Louis-Philippe (1814–30) as his successor.

[8] "The college of cardinals," writes Claude Barthe in *La tentation de Ralliement* (Paris: L'Homme Nouveau, 2022), 66, "was divided between the *zelanti*, the most intransigent defenders of the rights of the Church, and the *politicani*, moderates who argued for greater attention to modern political realities."

safeguard as much as possible of what remained of the religious life, the only line of diplomatic conduct that he could follow was to compromise with the hostile powers. Conversely, Lamennais considered that Christians could accept in principle the new states' lack of religious legitimacy, accepting what the authors of *Dignitatis Humanae*, and in particular the American Jesuit John Courtney Murray, later treated as self-evident, namely that the institutions of the State are in themselves neutral and have no jurisdiction in religious matters.

The same positions, but reversed, reappeared in the first period of the Second Empire.[9] The Catholic liberals, Charles de Montalembert and Félix Dupanloup, Bishop of Orléans, became opponents of the imperial regime, demanding a regime of civil and political liberties for which liberal and parliamentary Belgium furnished the model. The intransigents, on the other hand, following Louis Veuillot, greeted Napoléon III as a "new Charlemagne." They accepted without qualms the singing at the end of the Sunday high Mass of a triple *Domine, fac salvum imperatorem nostrum Napoleonem*,[10] and the inclusion in the Canon of the Mass of the "Christian" Emperor, after the pope and the bishop of the diocese. They would regret this error of judgment when they realized that the Emperor's Italian policy was greatly damaging to the interests of the pope. But the seriousness of their mistake resided not so much in their naïveté toward the new Bonaparte's easygoing Machiavellianism, as in their blindness toward the principles upon which the imperial regime was based, those of a bourgeois order, that is to say a liberal one.

One can continue the theme. How was Pius IX's successor, Leo XIII, able on the one hand to recall in

---

[9] The Second Empire, when Napoléon III was emperor, lasted from 1852–70. The earlier, more authoritarian period, is considered to have lasted from 1852–60. Veuillot was a journalist of strongly ultramontane views.

[10] "O Lord, save our emperor Napoléon."

the most uncompromising manner in his doctrinal pronouncements (the encyclical *Libertas Praestantissimum* of June 20, 1888, for example) that Catholics could not accept the modern conception of liberty, and on the other hand to say in the encyclical *Au Milieu des Sollicitudes* of February 16, 1892, that French Catholics should support "without hesitation" the regime founded on this same conception of liberty? And, another contradiction, this same Leo XIII, who invited French Catholics to support the Republic, forbade Italian Catholics—with his decree *Non Expedit* of February 29, 1868, and in line with the slogan *nè eletti, nè elettori* (neither elected nor electors)—to engage in the electoral process of the parliamentary monarchy founded by Cavour, who had stripped the Papacy of the Papal States. In reality, the diplomat pope was trying—quite naïvely, as events showed—to "twist" the laicism of the new European regimes to force them to catholicize themselves either by infiltration (the France of Émile Combes), or by impeding their functioning (the Italy of the House of Savoy).[11] This was a diplomatic policy that, so far as France was concerned, followed on from the Concordat of 1801, a convention to which both sides agreed in a spirit of realism: Napoléon, the heir of the Revolution, accepted the return of Catholic worship, while Pius VII granted Napoléon the right to nominate bishops, a right which the king had enjoyed before the "change of government," to use the euphemism with which the text of the Concordat referred to the Revolution. For Rome, this laboriously worked out compromise, immediately broken by Napoléon through

---

[11] Laicism (or laicity) is the political principle that the State should give no constitutional position to religious belief, which it consequently treats as an exclusively private matter. Émile Combes was *président du Conseil* 1902–1905 and a supporter of the 1905 law, separating the churches and the State. Victor Emmanuel II of the House of Savoy, from 1861 the first king of a united Italy, was behind the military campaigns against the Papal States which culminated in the capture of Rome in 1870.

the addition of the Seventy Seven Organic Articles further subordinating the Church to the State, seemed to be all that could be done to preserve Christ's kingly authority over France.

That is why Leo's successor, Pius X, a century later, in his encyclicals *Vehementer Nos*[12] and *Gravissimo officii munere*,[13] protested with all his strength against France's unilateral abrogation of the Concordat.[14] He made it clear that the principle of the separation of Church and State was undoubtedly deleterious:

> That the State must be separated from the Church is a thesis absolutely false, a most pernicious error. Based, as it is, on the principle that the State must not recognize any religious cult, it is in the first place guilty of a great injustice to God.... And if it is true that any Christian State does something eminently disastrous and reprehensible in separating itself from the Church, how much more deplorable is it that France, of all nations in the world, would have entered on this policy...[15]

But the Third Republic was in no sense a Christian state, and did not even resemble the states which feature in treatises on public ecclesiastical law and in the Church's Magisterium, states founded on the principles of natural law and legitimacy, the antithesis of Rousseau's social contract.[16] The 1905 Law of Separation therefore delivered the French Church from an unnatural wardship, if we are unreservedly to believe the doctrinal encyclicals of Leo XIII. It was moreover entirely in line with Leo's teaching that Pius X, who was more consistent in this

---

12 Pius X, Encyclical Letter *Vehementer Nos*, February 11, 1906.

13 Pius X, Encyclical Letter *Gravissimo officii munere*, August 10, 1906.

14 The concordat was abrogated by the 1905 Law of Separation.

15 Pius X, Encyclical Letter *Vehementer Nos*, February 11, 1906, nos. 3–4.

16 The Third Republic lasted from the collapse of the Second Empire in 1870 until 1940.

respect than his predecessor, broke with the previous tradition of a diplomatic approach: he forbade the French bishops, who were mostly in favor of compromise, to accept an inferior concordat, and in doing so he struck a blow against prominent Catholics such as Denys Cochin and Georges Goyau, who along with other academicians (the famous "green cardinals") had signed a letter calling for the Church to accept the establishment of the religious associations that the government was proposing.[17] Pius X did not want the French Church to commit itself by accepting the associations that the law was offering as a replacement of the system of the Concordat. That worked out well for him, since papal firmness led to a softening in the application of the law.[18] (Pius XI later removed the prohibition, considering that the original context of anti-clerical violence no longer held.)

Right up until Vatican II, official publications continued to discuss the legitimacy of human societies in terms of the "common good" which it was their duty to promote, as if the states to which these publications were addressed were capable of understanding this language, that is to say as if they admitted, at least implicitly, God's sovereignty over the public sphere. It is true that in its teaching Rome did take into consideration the ways things had developed and thus the dechristianization of societies. Magisterial pronouncements also developed the theme of the tolerance of non-Christian religious

---

[17] The letter of Cochin, Goyau, and others, "La Supplique aux Evêques," was published in *Le Figaro*, March 26, 1906. The authors were known as the "green cardinals" because eleven of the twenty three signatories were members of the *Institut Français* or of the *Académie Française*, distinguished by the green trimmings on their uniforms. The religious associations (*associations cultuelles*) would be able to own and maintain places of worship, and to organize worship in them, but would not be eligible for state aid.

[18] In 1923, following discussions between Raymond Poincaré, *président du Conseil*, and Msgr Bonaventura Cerretti, the papal nuncio, the Church was permitted to establish *associations diocésaines*, under the control of the diocesan bishop.

and philosophical opinions. This however referred above all to the tolerance that supposedly Christian legislators and governments should show to the propagation of false teaching: thus Leo XIII argued in his encyclical *Immortale Dei*, of November 1, 1885, that blocking the spread of error might lead to even greater problems than those consequent upon the free circulation of false teaching. The last to take this line was Pius XII, in his address to Catholic lawyers *Ci Riesce*:

> First: that which does not correspond to truth or to the norm of morality objectively has no right to exist, to be spread or to be activated. Secondly: failure to impede this with civil laws and coercive measures can nevertheless be justified in the interests of a higher and more general good.[19]

On the other hand, encyclicals rarely discussed how the Church was to exist in the face of a civil power which itself no longer had a transcendental reference point. "In the hope of some great good," as Leo XIII briefly put it, referring to a situation that was becoming universal, the Church "may show herself indulgent, and may conform to the times in so far as her sacred office permits."[20]

The ambiguous position of the Church of the *Syllabus* therefore derived entirely from the fact that she was giving instructions to modern states as if they were natural partners capable of understanding her teaching; so much so that her prophetic denunciations were little more than abstractions, a fact that papal diplomacy made all the more obvious. Thus Pius VII, after having magnificently stated the obligations of a civil power worthy of the title Christian in his encyclical *Diu Satis*, of May

---

19 Pius XII, Address to Catholic lawyers *Ci Riesce*, December 6, 1953, no. 5.

20 Leo XIII, Encyclical Letter *Libertas Praestantissimum*, June 20, 1888, no. 41.

15, 1800, came to Paris in 1804 to anoint the forehead of Bonaparte, the heir of the Revolution. The ceremony was expected to follow the model of the consecration of the Ancien Régime laid out in the Roman Pontifical,[21] with the one difference that Napoléon would vow to guarantee religious freedom in his states, thus taking the opposite position from that which had been proclaimed in Rheims.[22] It is true that a compromise was reached: Napoléon would make his vow immediately after the religious ceremony was thought to be over. Napoléon thus made his vow while the pope, who was processing out of the choir, could charitably be supposed not to have heard the vow at all.

A century and a half later, with greater discretion but in complete continuity with the earlier practice, the nuncio Angelo Roncalli, on being made a cardinal, conceived the idea that before leaving Paris he should recreate for President Vincent Auriol the privilege of the Most Christian Kings: on January 15, 1953, he knelt before the president to receive his cardinal's biretta at the president's hands.

---

[21] A pontifical is a service book containing rites and ceremonies performed by a bishop. The Roman Pontifical is the authoritative pontifical service book, based ultimately on the pontifical sections of the classic Roman liturgical books.

[22] French kings, at their coronations in Rheims Cathedral, swore to defend the Catholic faith.

CHAPTER 2

Catholic France in the 1950s

SIX YEARS LATER, on January 15, 1959, Roncalli, now Pope John XXIII, announced the summoning of the Second Vatican Council. When he had departed for his diocese of Venice as a newly appointed cardinal in February 1953, there had been nothing to suggest the earthquake that this announcement would trigger. This was however a superficial observation, since in the France that he had left as nuncio the ferment that would lead to the event of the Council was already in motion. Of course, one cannot deny the importance of the German or Dutch theologians of the decade which preceded and prepared for the Council, such as Karl Rahner (whose influence on Vatican II, transmitted by the German bishops, was immense), Hans Küng, and Edward Schillebeeckx. But France in the 1950s was a privileged arena in which clerics, engaged laymen, and bishops thought, in a characteristically chauvinist way, that they could settle the controversies of the entire Church. Rome, with a mixture of exasperation and of admiration for the genius of France and "her gifts of clarity and logical thought"[1] took a negative view of these ambitions: ever since the First World War—though this had been seen often enough in the past—the great issues that had occupied the Congregations headed by cardinals had been French issues (worker-priests,[2] progressive journals, the bringing into line of the Dominican provinces) and the sanctions, that is to say the silencings, in relative terms, which took place toward the end of the pontificate of Pius XII, principally

[1] Pius XII, Address to President René Coty of France, May 13, 1957.

[2] For the worker-priests, see p. 23, note 26.

targeted French theologians (Fathers Yves Congar, Marie-Dominique Chenu, Henri de Lubac, and Henri Bouillard).

Growth or Decline of the Church?—that was the question asked by Cardinal Emmanuel Suhard in his famous pastoral letter on the theme, "Neither Modernist nor Integrist."[3] He conceived the letter as a true encyclical, of value to the entire Church, something indicative of the state of mind of the French clergy. There was growth, if one considered the Church's internal dynamics: the healthy state of free secondary education, at least as regards the number of pupils, the success of the student movements and youth groups, themselves also growing in numerical terms, the great gatherings of the movements of *Action Catholique*, and the construction of churches in the suburbs (less artistic, however, and more functional than before the Second World War, because of the reduction in financial resources).[4] People congratulated themselves on the increased liturgical "participation," with a growth particularly in frequent Communion starting in 1955, thanks to the easing by Pius XII of the fasting requirement.

This internal revival, however, ran out of steam without any visible apostolic effects. The social shock caused by the war had considerably advanced the process of laicization. Dechristianization progressed, and in the middle of the 1960s we would start to see fragments of the Catholic world—the children of practicing families identifiable

---

[3] Cardinal Suhard, *Essor ou déclin de l'Église, Lettre pastorale* (Paris: Éditions A. Lahure, 1947), English translations by James A. Corbett, *Growth or Decline? The Church Today* (South Bend, IN: Fides, 1948) and Rev. Fr. Curry, *Rise or Decline of the Church* (London: Young Worker Publications for Young Christian Workers, 1949). The integrist (integralist, or integrationist) holds that even though Church and State have separate spheres of operation, they are both ultimately subject to the overlordship of Christ, and should therefore in some areas work together with a view to the common good.

[4] *Action Catholique* is an umbrella term for a number of lay Catholic evangelical associations, such as *Jeunesse Ouvrière Catholique*, *Association Catholique de la Jeunesse Française*, *Jeunesse Étudiante Chrétienne*, and *Jeunesse Étudiante Chrétienne Féminine*.

up until then by their Catholic activities, the country people, the provinces of the West—detach themselves from religious practice.

At this point we need to take a step back. These decisive years can really only be understood in continuity with the inter-war period, the time of what has been called the "Second *Ralliement*."[5] Both the strategy of adaptation to the modern world, which seemed to have been programmed into the French Church of the 1950s, and the great debates over mission to a dechristianizing society followed on directly from what had been done, said, or written during the pontificate of Pius XI. There is an eye-witness account of the France of this period, indeed a deeply committed and passionate account, in the work of Georges Bernanos, one of the Catholic authors of the generation which began its work before the Second World War, that of Paul Claudel, Joseph Malègue, and Julien Green. It would be no great exaggeration to say that the two great polemical works of this born adversary of the Church's every compromise with the modern world, *La grande peur des bien-pensants* and *Les grands cimetières sous la lune*, are essentially directed the former at Leo XIII, and the latter at Pius XI, the popes behind the two *Ralliements*.[6]

The central focus of this novelist and polemicist was entirely characteristic of the period. From 1925 the pessimists gained ground over the optimists. It was a season of clarity, a clarity which the investigations of Gabriel Le Bras and Canon Fernand Boulard would reinforce.[7] Long

---

[5] Adrien Dansette, *Histoire religieuse de la France contemporaine*, vol. 2, *Sous la IIIème République* (Paris: Flammarion, 1950), abridged English trans. by John Dingle, *Religious History of Modern France*, vol. 2, *Under the Third Republic* (Freiburg: Herder; Edinburgh: Nelson, 1961).

[6] Georges Bernanos, *La grande peur des bien-pensants* (Paris: F. Paillart, 1931); *Les grands cimetières sous la lune* (Paris: les petits-fils de Plon et Nourrit, 1938).

[7] Gabriel Le Bras, *Introduction à l'histoire de la pratique religieuse en France*, 2 vols. (Paris: Presses universitaires de France, 1942–45); *Études de sociologie religieuse*, 2 vols. (Paris: Presses universitaires de France, 1955–56); Fernand Boulard, *Essor ou déclin du clergé français?*

before the book of the Abbés Godin and Daniel, *France pays de mission?*, studies, books, such as *Le Faubourg* and *La Menace rouge* of Jacques Valdour, and *Pêcheurs d'hommes* of Maxence Van der Meersch, investigations, articles, all hammered home the themes of the "paganization of the masses."[8] Bernanos's work is among those which cast light on the realization of the "death of God," and the attempt to describe and analyze it, since Bernanos was a contemporary of Dietrich Bonhoeffer and of Sigmund Freud's *The Future of an Illusion*. There is a sense of distress that runs through Bernanos's novels, distress at a vanishing Christianity. "My parish is eaten up by boredom—there, I have used the word—like so many other parishes! Boredom is consuming them in front of our eyes," says the Country Curé, who adds, "and we can't do anything about it."[9] Christian priests, whether mystics or down-to-earths, stand by helplessly at this death by consumption. Bernanos's great novel, *Monsieur Ouine*, is the story of a "dead parish," emptied of all Christian substance.[10] That will soon be the fate of all the parishes of France. The universe which surrounds Ouine, the teacher of corruption, is the modern world such as Bernanos sees it, a world of souls without love, who have become wholly estranged from the message of Redemption.

Nevertheless everything that Bernanos wrote on this subject stands out from the prevailing view, perhaps

---

(Paris: Cerf, 1950); *Carte religieuse de la France rurale* (Paris: Cahiers du clergé rural, 1952).

[8] Henri Godin and Yvan Daniel, *La France, pays de mission?* (Lyon: Éd. de l'Abeille, 1943); Jacques Valdour [pseudonym of Louis Martin], *Le faubourg, observations vécues* (Paris: Éd. Spes, 1925); *La Menace rouge, ouvriers d'après guerre en Touraine* (Paris: Gazette française, 1926); Maxence Van der Meersch, *Pêcheurs d'hommes* (Paris: A. Michel, 1940), English translations *Fishers of Men* (London: Miles, 1947); *Fishers of Men* (London: Geoffrey Chapman, 1957).

[9] Bernanos, *Journal d'un curé de campagne* (Paris: Plon, 1936), English trans. by Pamela Morris, *The Diary of a Country Priest* (London: Bodley Head, 1937).

[10] Bernanos, *Monsieur Ouine* (Paris: Plon, 1946), English trans. by Geoffrey Dunlop, *The Open Mind* (London: John Lane, 1945).

because of the excess of his mordant style—he identifies, in *La Grande Peur des bien-pensants*, "the change, perhaps already beyond cure, of Man's religious sense"—but above all because of his assignation of blame. Very quickly, he saw that the bloodshed of the Great War had not changed what was at stake in the political world, and that on the contrary the old world was always there, unchanged. We are again face to face with idols, as described in the title of a book by his friend, Robert Vallery-Radot, *Devant les idoles.*[11] In the vision of Bernanos, the victims of the modern world, which triumphs through a godless democracy, following which man no longer looks toward anything outside himself, are the little people, the great mass of the weak, in whom even the root of hope has been twisted out of shape. Who is to blame? First of all, those who admitted defeat, the Catholic leaders who reneged on their prophetic duty to denounce the modern state. Bernanos criticized François Mauriac for taking refuge in a literature devoted to Man's interior state and had him say, "Restore Christianity, that vast medieval fraternity?—what an absurd idea!" Bernanos accused Jacques Maritain of inspiring a general retreat into the sacristies in pursuit of the "primacy of the spiritual."[12] As he moved from pamphlet to article in his fight against the bien-pensants, Bernanos's breast swelled with fighting spirit as he confronted "the church leaders who are responsible," who speak the language of "*sang-froid* and prudence." "Speaking like that," he said, "is truly to abandon hope for Christianity. It is to expel the flower of our people from Christianity."[13]

---

[11] Robert Vallery-Radot, *Devant les idoles* (Paris: Perrin et Cie, 1921).

[12] Bernanos was responding to Jacques Maritain, *Primauté du spirituel* (Paris: Plon, 1927), English trans. by J. F. Scanlan, *The Things That are Not Caesar's* (London: Sheed & Ward, 1939). Jacques Maritain (1882–1973) converted to Catholicism in 1906 and applied a Thomist perspective to a wide range of contemporary topics.

[13] Bernanos, *Nous autres Français* (Paris: Gallimard, 1939), 142–44.

When Bernanos denounced the Spanish Civil War, in which the blood of the poor was so profusely shed, it was the clergy whom he accused, the Spanish bishops, the Roman diplomats, those who supported the *Movimento Nacional* for the same reasons, according to Bernanos, as they had previously forced the Spanish Church to support the republic under the banner of the *Acción Popular* of Gil Robles (even so, it seems that the massacres of religious and the pillage of the churches by the Reds created a new situation).[14] Never directly named, but always the ultimate focus, was the pope. Bernanos is sure, as passionately sure as he can be, that Pius XI really was the pope of the Second *Ralliement* of French Catholicism, a *Ralliement* that was much more successfully pursued than that of Leo XIII, a restoration of diplomatic relations between the Vatican and the French Republic, allowing a calmer outlook within the Church, which abandoned all unspoken thoughts of questioning the regime's legitimacy (Rome did not at all appreciate the exceptionally combative declaration of the Assembly of Cardinals and Archbishops in 1925); condemnation of the trouble-makers of *Action Française* (even if the condemnation was originally for doctrinal issues, it was the independent attitude of Charles Maurras toward the instructions from Rome that exasperated Pius XI); a policy of nominating bishops hostile to integrism; and a reduction in the militant activity under the aegis of *Action Catholique* (General Castelnau's independent *Fédération Nationale Catholique* was deeply critical of a section of the French bishops and of Rome).[15]

---

[14] José María Gil Robles founded the right-wing Catholic party *Acción Popular* in 1931, and subsequently led the *Confederación Española de Derechos Autónomos* (CEDA). Following the success of CEDA in the elections of November 1933, he was briefly Minister for War in 1935, but after the Civil War he went into exile in Portugal.

[15] The cardinals' and archbishops' *Déclaration sur les lois dites de la laïcité et les mesures à prendre pour les combattre*, March 10, 1925, condemned laicism and called on Catholics to declare war on

Bernanos, therefore, despite his exaggerations and lack of restraint, never ceased to put his finger on this wound which would become still more evident after 1945: the Church "has dedicated all its intellect, all its strength, to the creation of a minimal Christianity, of a caricature of Christianity, this clerical party, this party of bien-pensants, whose essential and incurable mediocrity, revealed in politics as well as in art, astonishes and scandalizes men of good will."[16]

Conversely, if it was Bernanos who cursed the 1930s, it was Jacques Maritain in his later period, that of the writings following the condemnation of *Action Française*, who was not the inspiration of the period but its intellectual point of reference. In a certain sense, therefore, when Maritain translated into laymen's terms Pius XI's teaching in *Quas Primas* on the subject of Christ the King, he played the same role that Dupanloup had played in the nineteenth century, in translating the *Syllabus* into laymen's terms. There is nevertheless a significant difference: Maritain was acting not only with the approval of Pius XI but practically on his instructions. Pius XI himself interpreted the restoration of the reign of Christ the King, the arrival of what people used to call a "new Christianity," as a baptism of democracy: the pope dreamed of Christianizing first and foremost the Italian parliamentary system, and if possible the other European democracies, through the organization of a network of Catholic associations and particularly through the influence of *Action Catholique*.

---

laicism and its principles. *Action Française*, a political rather than a religious movement, was founded in 1899 and in its early years was dominated by Charles Maurras, a royalist who though personally a freethinker supported the Catholic Church. General Castelnau, whose *Fédération Nationale Catholique* held its first congress in 1925, was fiercely Catholic and patriotic.

[16] Frédéric Lefèvre, "Une heure avec Bernanos," in *Les Nouvelles littéraires*, May 9, 1931; reprinted in Georges Bernanos, *Essais et écrits de combat*, ed. Michel Estève, et al., vol. 1 (Paris: Gallimard, 1971), 1217–23.

The ingenious distinction that Maritain had established in *Humanisme intégral*, between the "sacral" Christianity of the Middle Ages and a "profane" Christianity—that is to say, a pluralist society into which Christians somehow breathe the spirit of the gospel—nevertheless succeeded in reinvigorating, though in a minor mode, the themes of integrism.[17] "We want France to see a great return of Christianity," sang the members of the *Jeunesse Ouvrière Catholique* in the stadium of the *Parc des Princes* at the time, in 1937.[18] Today's traditionalists, ardent supporters of the liturgical feast of Christ the King, would be astonished if they were to be told that it was above all the feast of *Action Catholique*.

Maritain's project was nothing other than a revival of liberal Catholicism: not so much a distinction between thesis and hypothesis, with the thesis being dispatched to the clouds, as a spiritualization of the thesis. And yet, in practice, this project had fallen behind the progress of the *Ralliement* in the heart of French Catholicism: in reality, within the ranks of Catholicism, *Primauté du spirituel* and *Humanisme intégral* enabled a settling of accounts with *Action Française* and the Catholic integrists, but failed completely to inspire a strategy of political reconquest. Paul Archambault, philosopher and disciple of Maurice Blondel, and Blondel himself, both of them fervent democrats, were much more representative of the dominant current in French Catholicism than Maritain, a Thomist and Maurrasian who had only arrived at democracy after making some subtle distinctions (it would be 1945 before he really completed the transition). No matter: the word *chrétienté*—or Christendom—remained part of Catholic political vocabulary until the Second World

[17] Jacques Maritain, *Humanisme intégral: problèmes temporels et spirituels d'une nouvelle chrétienté* (Paris: Fernand Aubier, 1936), English trans. by Margot Robert Adamson, *True Humanism*, 2nd ed. (New York: Scribner, 1938).

[18] Quoted by Yvon Tranvouez in *Catholiques d'abord, approches du mouvement catholique en France, XIXe–XXe siècle* (Paris: Éd. Ouvrières, 1988).

War. Monsignor Bruno de Solages, rector of the Catholic Institute of Toulouse, wrote a work entitled *Pour rebâtir une chrétienté*, and entrusted the concrete realization of the project to his friend Georges Bidault.[19]

However, after 1945—and that is the period which is the focus of this chapter and on which this return to the inter-war period is intended to shed light—Maritain's philosophico-political work seemed in France to have lost its value. In Italy it became one of the points of reference of the Christian Democracy which came to power, a useful point of reference since its subtle distinctions allowed a theoretical *combinazione* between the papal anti-modern teaching, still in force, and the democratic reality. But in the France of the Fourth Republic, which despite the presence of the *Mouvement Républicain Populaire* was infinitely more secularized, no one paid serious attention to this aspect of Maritain's work.[20] Was the French Church engaged in a project? Did it even have a political philosophy? The French cardinals of that period were democratic prelates whom Pius XI had named as bishops after 1926—Cardinal Feltin, named in 1927, Cardinal Liénart, in 1928, Cardinal Gerlier, in 1929, and Cardinal Richaud, in 1933—to counteract the tendency of those close to Catholic integrism whom Pius X had named as bishops after the Separation. These new bishops would govern the destiny of the French Church until the time of the Council, and for them political engagement was reduced to the defense of the *école libre*.

---

[19] Bruno de Solages, *Pour rebâtir une chrétienté* (Paris: Éditions Spes, 1939). Georges Bidault, a former member of the resistance, occupied several ministerial posts after the Second World War, and was briefly *Président du Conseil* in 1949–50. He parted company with De Gaulle over Algeria.

[20] The post-war Fourth Republic lasted from 1946–58. It was dissolved following De Gaulle's return to power. The *Mouvement Républicain Populaire*, founded in 1944, was a conservative Christian Democrat movement. It was particularly successful in the elections of 1946.

Weakened in their authority because of the support that they had given the Vichy regime, these bishops now merely showed a paternal indulgence toward these new libertarian trends. The brakes were worn, and the machine raced away. In France the 1950s were a period of vast and explosive debates: over the experiment of the worker-priests; over the evolutionism of Father Teilhard de Chardin, whose works circulated "under the counter," in the time-honored expression, which meant in practice in Roneo-typed form, in the full view and full knowledge of everyone; over the criticism of the scholastic method by the theological schools of Fourvière (Jesuits from Lyon) and of Saulchoir (Dominicans from Paris), whom we will meet again;[21] over the progressivism of Catholics who were fascinated in different ways by Marxism, along with the journals *Esprit*, *Témoignage chrétien*, *La Quinzaine*—founded in 1950 around Father Maurice Montuclard, and forcibly closed by a decree of the Holy Office in 1955[22]—and *L'Actualité religieuse dans le monde* (founded in 1953, and transformed in 1955 into *Informations catholiques internationales*). That was the period which saw the internal crisis of the youth wing of *Action Catholique*, split between the *Jeunesse Ouvrière Catholique*, which focused on the industrial world, and the generalist *Association Catholique de la Jeunesse Française*, and during which the divisions over the Algerian question broke out: in May 1957 the national leaderships of *La Route* (senior scouts),

[21] The intellectual and analytic scholastic method is that followed by the scholastics, or the practitioners of scholasticism, that is to say, the search for a deeper understanding of revealed truth by means of philosophical speculation. More specifically, this group of terms refers to the philosophical and theological developments associated with authors such as St Thomas Aquinas.

[22] The Holy Office was a Roman Congregation established in 1542 as the final court of appeal in cases of heresy, and was of considerable importance in doctrinal matters. It has been reconstituted more recently and is now the Dicastery for the Doctrine of the Faith, the final court dealing with issues of faith or morals.

of the *Jeunesse Étudiante Chrétienne*, and of the *Jeunesse Étudiante Chrétienne Féminine* resigned in protest against the support which the hierarchy was then giving to the army. The pot was boiling.

The same period saw a continuation of a process of theological and spiritual growth which had started during the preceding period, but was from now on entangled with the opening symptoms of the crisis. The only topic of discussion was "renewal": liturgical renewal (*La vie de la liturgie*, by Louis Bouyer, the journal *La Maison-Dieu* of the *Centre de Pastorale Liturgique*, which became the *Centre National de Pastorale Liturgique* in 1965); patristic renewal (Jean Daniélou, Claude Mondésert); theological renewal (Henri de Lubac, Hans Urs von Balthasar, Marie-Dominique Chenu); ecumenical renewal (Yves Congar); artistic renewal (the journal *L'Art Sacré*, of Fathers Marie-Alain Régamey and Pie Couturier, whose golden period ran from 1945 to 1955); and biblical renewal, which nevertheless remained restrained until the time of the Council. Vatican II, for example, had already started when Xavier Léon Dufour published his *Les Évangiles et l'histoire de Jésus*, with its Christological interpretations that prompted scandal.[23]

This combination of deeper intellectual exploration and criticism, at least in moderate tones, of everything that had gone before, was particularly exemplified by the flowering of new study-texts for seminarians and theological students: the *Introduction à la Bible*, by Fathers André Robert and André Feuillet; *La Loi du Christ*, by Father Bernhard Häring; the *Initiation théologique*, edited by Father Antonin-Marcel Henry; the *Initiation aux Pères de l'Église*, by Father Johannes Quasten; *L'Église en prière*, by Father Aimé-Georges Martimort; and of course the

[23] Louis Bouyer, *La vie de la liturgie: une critique constructive du Mouvement liturgique* (Paris: Cerf, 1956); Xavier Léon-Dufour, *Les Évangiles et l'histoire de Jésus* (Paris: Seuil, 1963), English trans. by John McHugh, *The Gospels and the Jesus of History* (London: Collins, 1968).

Jerusalem Bible.[24] The training of the clergy seemed to be of the highest quality. Yet it was the classes of seminarians trained during these years which were to a great extent cut down between 1965 and 1970 by the departures from the priesthood. The classes were in fact deeply marked by a crisis mentality. They were given the worst of supports to enable them to start on a career that was in human terms less and less rewarding, supports consisting merely in the doubts and irresolution of the teachers in their institutions. The drop in vocations continued, though it did not match the collapse which took place after the Council: the ordinations in the dioceses of France, which had increased after the war thanks to the arrival of vocations held up by the *service du travail obligatoire* or by captivity in Germany,[25] went on to fall from 820 to 655 between 1955 and 1965. Growth or decline? Even before the Council, a certain number of diocesan seminaries were preparing to close.

---

[24] A. Robert and A. Feuillet (eds.), *Introduction à la Bible* (Paris: Desclée, 1957), English trans. by Patrick W. Skehan, *Introduction to the New Testament* (New York: Desclée, 1965); Bernard Hăring, *Das Gesetz Christi. Moraltheologie. Dargestellt für Priester und Laien* (Freiburg: Erich Wewel Verlag, 1954), French trans. by F. Bourdeau, A. Danet, and L. Vereecke, *La Loi du Christ: théologie morale à l'intention des prêtres et des laïcs*, 3 vols. (Paris: Desclée et Cie, 1957–59), English trans. by Edwin G. Kaiser, *The Law of Christ, Moral Theology for Priests and Laity*, 3 vols. (Cork: Mercier Press, 1963–67); *Initiation théologique*, by a group of theologians, 4 vols. (Paris: Cerf, 1952–54); Johannes Quasten, *Patrology*, 4 vols. (Utrecht: Spectrum; Westminster, MD: Newman Press, 1949–60), French trans. by J. Laporte, *Initiation aux Pères de l'Église*, 4 vols. (Paris: Cerf, 1955–87); A. G. Martimort, *L'Église en prière: introduction à la liturgie* (Paris: Desclée, 1961), English trans. of new ed., *The Church at Prayer*, 4 vols. (Collegeville, MN: Liturgical Press, 1986–88); *La Sainte Bible*, trans. École biblique de Jérusalem (Paris: Club français du livre, 1955–56), English version, Alexander Jones (ed.), *The Jerusalem Bible* (London: Darton, Longman and Todd, 1966).

[25] The *service du travail obligatoire* (Compulsory Work Service) was a scheme under which from 1943 the German occupying forces in France called up French citizens for compulsory work in Germany. At the end of the war there were about 700,000 Frenchmen working in Germany under this scheme.

Typical of the religious projects of this period were those aimed at the working class, the *Mission de France*, the *Mission de Paris*, and above all the apostolate of the worker-priests.[26] From now on no one spoke any longer as they had done previously about "reconquest" (an attempt at conquest would have been more appropriate, given that ever since Adrien Dansette it has been a commonplace that the working class, at least in the Paris region, is born dechristianized), but about "bearing witness," about a silent presence, like leaven buried in dough. Gilbert Cesbron's novel, *Les saints vont en enfer*, reveals the sentimental view of the factory experience of the priests taken by a good part of the clergy and faithful.[27] A frisson of scandalized pleasure ran through "advanced" Catholics when they thought about these consecrated men who wore a flat cap and said Mass at a kitchen table.

The basic question raised by the worker-priests was nevertheless crucial. If the worker-priests and the theologians who supported them displayed an immense naïveté when faced with the "industrial civilization," which concealed the reality of the communist *Confédération Générale du Travail*, their naïveté was matched by that of the French bishops, who looked on the experience as no different from that of the charitable works to which they were accustomed: such works should above all never have any aim of political change either to the right or to the left.[28] The French bishops were most worried by the compatibility between work in a factory and priestly spirituality:

---

[26] The worker-priest movement was intended to reconnect the French Catholic Church with manual workers. Taking their cue from clandestine priests who had joined French workers deported to Germany during the war, worker-priests took up employment in factories and similar locations. The project was brought to a halt by papal intervention in the 1950s.

[27] Gilbert Cesbron, *Les Saints vont en enfer* (Paris: R. Laffont, 1952), English trans. by John Russell, *Saints in Hell* (London: Secker & Warburg, 1953).

[28] The *Confédération Générale du Travail*, founded in 1895, is one of France's principal trade unions.

"Do they still pray their breviary?" asked Cardinal Suhard, without realizing that the issue was entirely different, and involved a much deeper issue. Much more than a simple relationship formed by toiling alongside workers who were often communists, an idea was making its way forward, which would go a long way toward bringing about the acceptance of the "extended hand," the idea that Christianity is powerless against Marxism.

The experiment of the worker-priests would certainly have ended in failure, even if, in November 1953, Rome had not imposed multiple conditions, including a ban on working full-time in a factory, thus requiring the French bishops to bring it to an almost complete halt. But the ambition of the worker-priests, or at any rate of some of them, which they shared with a section of the progressive movement, was by no means to be despised: it focused on transforming social and political structures in order to allow the effective preaching of Christ. It was linked to what is generally described as "integrism," that is to say an all-embracing religious vision governing the entirety of social life, but in this case an integrism of the left. It was this integrism, much more than a sympathetic attitude to communism, which shocked the naïve liberalism of the parishioners who attended Sunday Mass, who had early suspected the bishops of being "socialist" and who were shocked by Pius XI's encyclical *Quadragesimo Anno* of May 15, 1931, which was as much anti-capitalist as it was anti-Marxist: "What," they asked, "is the pope getting himself involved in?"

In reality, the French bishops quite naturally came to accept the liberalism of French society, which was becoming deeply rooted. That explains why the French cardinals and bishops—with just a few exceptions, such as the concerns expressed by Monsignor Xavier Morilleau, Bishop of La Rochelle—were able to say on September 17, 1958, that there was no reason for concern in the fact that the projected constitution of the Fifth

Republic referred to the *Declaration of the Rights of Man* of 1789, to the laicity of the Republic, and to the principle that the State should give equal respect to all religious beliefs.[29] Catholics could calm their conscience, said the bishops, by understanding laicity as meaning that the State respects all religions, rather than that it is in principle hostile to Christianity. An additional reason for the bishops to adopt this position, which seemed to them completely obvious, was that it enabled them to reply to the strongly-argued criticisms of the constitution coming from the Catholic "integrist" circles.

If influential French Catholic circles had taken even the slightest interest in the internal debates among the Italian clerico-political class, which took place at about the same time in the shadow of the Lateran Pacts,[30] they would have thought them mad. For example, on the other side of the Alps Italian legal writers were questioning Pius XI's successor, Pius XII, (it was this that prompted his address to Catholic lawyers, mentioned above) over whether a Catholic politician or a Catholic state was allowed to join a "Community of Peoples" or a confederation which admitted the principle of religious pluralism. Pius XII was developing the anti-modern papal Magisterium of the nineteenth and twentieth centuries, beginning from the principle, "that which does not correspond to truth or to the norm of morality objectively has no right to exist, to be spread or to be activated." But in the Catholic France of the 1950s, this papal teaching now seemed realistic only to relatively marginal journals,

---

[29] "Les cardinaux de France déclarent . . . " (*Le Monde*, September 18, 1958).

[30] The Lateran Pacts were a group of three agreements between the Vatican and the Italian state, signed on February 11, 1929. The Lateran Treaty established the Vatican as a sovereign state; the Concordat safeguarded the Catholic position in Italy in areas such as marriage and education; and the Financial Convention compensated the Vatican for those portions of the Papal States lost during the unification of Italy.

theologians, and currents of thought (such as *La pensée catholique* of Abbés Luc Lefèvre and Henri Lusseau).

In France, unlike Italy, everyone's reflections were focused on the religious pluralism mentioned in the question which the legal writers put to Pius XII. But these reflections were completely different from the concerns of the Roman school of theology, which looked at pluralism as an aspect of toleration. In France, the angle from which the question was addressed was already that of ecumenism, which implicitly admitted the concept of a religious dialogue based on the equality of the participants. It was moreover this way of considering the question of religious pluralism which was to spearhead the great about-turn which was already in the making.

CHAPTER 3

Ecumenism and the "True Reform of the Church"

THE ECUMENICAL PROJECT was not solely the product of the thought of Yves Congar, the best-known French theologian of the pre-conciliar period. Nevertheless, Congar was a pioneer and his thought remains unsurpassed to this day. In fact it is in a true sense unsurpassable, in that it is precisely poised over the fine dividing line between dogma and its opposite.

As we examine Congar's theological explorations, we need to recall that he mapped their outlines during the pontificate of Pius XI, in the inter-war period, and that he developed them fully, despite several "sanctions," in the favorable and excited atmosphere of the 1950s. We can keep in mind two dates: 1937 (Congar, who had been teaching at Saulchoir for six years, was thirty-three), the year of publication of *Chrétiens désunis, Principes d'un "oecuménisme" catholique*, a book in which we find the original inspiration for the documents of Vatican II that covered the principles of ecumenism (the constitution *Lumen Gentium* and the decree *Unitatis Redintegratio*) and which was the first volume in the collection *Unam Sanctam*, founded by Congar with the publisher Cerf; and 1950 (when Congar was forty-six), the year of publication of *Vraie et fausse réforme dans l'Église*, a work which contains the key to the adoption of these principles as norms for action, that is to say, the relegation of the dogmatic function to a glass display case.[1]

[1] Yves Congar, *Chrétiens désunis: Principes d'un "oecuménisme" catholique* (Paris: Cerf, 1937), English trans. by M. A. Bousfield,

Of course, Congar is not the only person to whom we should assign the paternity of these two aspects of the project, particularly of the second, which owes much to the victory of the *nouvelle théologie* over the classic principles of both theology and the Magisterium. Yet this Dominican was endowed with an obvious charisma. He had a brilliant mind, he was an excellent teacher in French as in Latin, he spoke with an easy fluency, he had read everything and he had thought everything through, he wrote in a style that was simple and without any affectation that might suggest a lack of seriousness, he "conspired" in broad daylight, or almost, against the Roman School, he was easy to approach and displayed a sincere openness to all, he was plunged sometimes into despair, but liable also to flights of enthusiasm, and his doctrinal influence on the Council, starting from the second session, was considerable. He did not cease running courses, giving lectures, writing notes, publishing books, articles, summaries, prefaces for other books, contributing to debates, seminars, dictionaries, and collective works. His bibliography is vast. It does not however abound in every direction: he devoted much the greater part of his labor to ecclesiology, always directing attention toward the front line of ecumenism.

The origin of ecumenism lies in Protestantism. Catholicism has certainly always had a concern for unity with separated Christians, but it sought to realize that unity in the form of a reintegration of the separated Christians into the Church which they themselves or their fathers had left. In addition to the pastoral approach focused on the return of individuals, much effort has been made to obtain collective reunions: the Second Council of Lyons (1274) led to an act of union with the Greeks, and the Council of

---

Divided Christendom: A Catholic Study of the Problem of Reunion (London: Geoffrey Bles, 1939); *Vraie et fausse réforme dans l'Église* (Paris: Cerf, 1950), English trans. by Paul Philibert, *True and False Reform in the Church* (Collegeville, MN: Liturgical Press, 2011).

Florence (1430) led to acts of union with several oriental Churches. In both cases the reunions were short-lived, but other reunions, partial or global, have given rise to the so-called Uniate Churches. People used the word "uniatism" to describe these reunions, or "unionism" to describe more generally the totality of efforts to obtain the reunion of groups of non-Catholic Christians, including the groups arising from the Protestant reform.

Ecumenism emerged in Protestant pietist circles in the eighteenth century, but it first acquired a formal existence at the start of the twentieth century, at the 1910 Edinburgh World Missionary Conference, attended by delegates from eight hundred Christian communities, including some Orthodox Churches. In 1948 the movement gave birth to the World Council of Churches (WCC). The most important ecclesiological statement of the WCC (which did not include the Orthodox) was that of Toronto, in July 1950, entitled, *The Church, the Churches, and the World Council of Churches*. This was a sort of charter: each member Church was free to assert its own ecclesiological teaching. Membership "does not imply that a Church treats its own conception of the Church as merely relative." But this affirmation was itself relative since it added that "the point of the ecumenical conversation was precisely that all these conceptions enter into dynamic relations with each other," with the single Church of Christ transcending confessional boundaries.[2] In 1961 the Section on Unity of the WCC proposed this ecumenical resolution to the General Assembly, as "dynamic" as it was imprecise:

> We believe that the unity which is both God's will and his gift to his Church is being made visible as all in each place who are baptized into Jesus Christ and confess him as Lord and Savior

[2] WCC Central Committee, *The Church, the Churches, and the World Council of Churches: The Ecclesiological Significance of the World Council of Churches* (New York: WCC, 1953), 8.

> are brought by the Holy Spirit into one fully committed fellowship, holding the one apostolic faith, preaching the one Gospel, breaking the one bread...[3]

So far as Protestantism, in its totality, with its multiple variations and emphases, is concerned, the Church is above all an invisible community of those who believe in the faith, while their ecclesial institutions can vary substantially according to their socio-cultural contexts. This inevitably caused difficulties for the Orthodox, who until 1969 always made separate statements. As for the Catholic Church, she could not consent to this charter, and she has never joined the WCC, even after the Council, contenting herself with sending observers.

Two different views of the position of the different Churches therefore stood opposed to each other: for non-Catholic ecumenism, until such time as unity comes about, we have to deal with Churches which are all imperfect (each one of them, for its part, regarding itself as less imperfect than the others); for Catholic ecumenism, strictly speaking, only one Church, the Catholic Church, has the right to the title Church. And, as is logical, there are the same two views over the manner of achieving unity: for non-Catholic ecumenism, unity will develop, so to speak, "in advance," in the Church of Christ with which no existing Church can claim to fully identify itself; for Catholic ecumenism, which does not deny the existence of *vestigia ecclesiae*, that is to say elements of the Church outside the Roman communion (and sometimes very important elements, as can be seen in the case of Orthodoxy), unity can come about only by means of the re-integration into the Church of those who have left her. In accordance with this traditional view, the projected council examined by Pius XII, of which we

---

[3] *The New Delhi Report: The Third Assembly of the World Council of Churches* (London: SCM, 1962), 116. The translator is grateful to Lyn van Rooyen of the WCC for this reference.

will speak below, included a solemn declaration inviting non-Catholic Christians to "return to the common table."

Unity without return or unity by return of the separated to the Church of Peter? From the start, this was the cross on which Catholic ecumenism suffered. On the one hand, it had to avoid reduction to the first alternative, the ecumenism of the WCC, the adoption of which would have been to stray into heresy. Equally it had to avoid a reduction to uniatism, and more particularly a uniatism whose structure allowed the re-integrated communities to preserve important disciplinary and liturgical features of their own. If one was going to create a Catholic ecumenism, between the Catholic understanding of unity and the Protestant, the third way seemed *a priori* to be the pursuit of a chimera.

The first Catholic attempts at ecumenical conversations, which took place with the Anglicans, naturally revolved around this question. These began with conversations in Madeira between Father Fernand Portal and the Anglican Lord Halifax in 1889. Initially encouraged by Leo XIII, the *Revue anglo-romaine* of Portal, which was keeping the conversations going, ceased publication after the apostolic letter *Apostolicae Curae* of September 13, 1896, in which the pope declared Anglican orders null. Other discussions then took place at the request of Portal and Halifax—the famous Malines Conversations—between various Catholic and Anglican historians and theologians, from 1921 to 1926, under the aegis of Cardinal Désiré Mercier, Archbishop of Malines. A critical pause came when Mercier read a document drawn up by the Benedictine Dom Lambert Beauduin, concerning the possible re-attachment to Rome of an Anglican Church "united but not absorbed." The document taken up by Mercier proposed a return without a return, in a manner of speaking, which was silent about Anglican ordinations and the dogmas that the Anglicans did not accept. Mercier and Portal were already dead when Pius XI, in his encyclical *Mortalium Animos*, gave the supporters of ecumenism the equivalent of a cold shower: "the union of Christians can only be promoted by promoting the return to the one true Church of Christ of those who are separated from it, for in the past they have unhappily left it."[4]

Congar made his appearance on the grand theological stage nine years later, at the end of the Pius XI's pontificate, in 1937, when he returned to the ideas of the pioneers. *Chrétiens désunis* made a powerful contribution to the spread of ecumenical ideas in Catholic circles, but went out of print in 1941 and was only re-issued in 1965. It narrowly escaped condemnation and thereafter, and until the end of the succeeding pontificate of Pius XII, Congar took the greatest care to avoid any new writing on the subject of "formal ecumenism," to use his own expression, or in other words containing any theological exposition of the principles of ecumenism.

The central thesis of the book was to be found in the seventh chapter, "The Status of Our Separated Brethren." This chapter contained two examples of a form of reasoning typical of Congar, that is to say, the juxtaposition of an assertion quite unacceptable as it stands from a Catholic point of view and a theological proposition perfectly classical in form, with each "nuancing" the other. At the start, therefore, in the case of the non-Catholic Churches, the distinction between being and having was completely blurred.

First proposition: "[The non-conforming Churches] are to different degrees elements of the Church" (or in other words, the sociological reality of Lutheranism is an element of the true Church),[5] an affirmation that in itself is heterodox.

---

[4] Pius XI, Encyclical Letter *Mortalium Animos*, January 6, 1928, no. 10.

[5] Congar here uses the phrase "non-conforming churches" to denote non-Catholic denominations which declined to accept the authority of the Papal magisterium.

Second proposition: "They have more or less preserved elements or principles productive of the one Church" (nobody really disputes that Lutheranism has the sacrament of baptism and certain truths of the faith), a proposition that is entirely acceptable.

There then followed another juxtaposition to which the response is "yes and no."

First proposition: the separated faithful sanctify themselves "not despite their denomination, but in and through their denomination" (or in other words, a Calvinist sanctifies himself through the evangelical Church to which he belongs).

Second proposition: "it is really despite their denomination that souls sanctify themselves in their denomination" (everyone agrees, in reality, that a Calvinist of good faith can eventually sanctify himself by the means of the true Church even if he stays, apparently, as a matter of fact, in the bosom of heresy).

In this fog of words, the ultimate end of ecumenism escaped the reader's grasp: the terms "return" and *a fortiori* "recantation" were carefully avoided, in favor of "reunion of Churches," "integration," and the "fulfilment" of the principles of communion which exist in the separated communities.

In 1950 Congar brought out his principal work, *Vraie et fausse réforme dans l'Église*. The fundamental theme was substantially the same as that which liberal Catholicism had been debating for a century and a half: "reconciling the Church and a particular form of the modern world." Congar, like Monsignor Maret, thought that this could not be achieved simply by introducing modern ideas into the Church just as they were, but that "work in depth" was required first. Through this labor the permanent principles of Catholicism would develop anew while assimilating certain specific insights of modernity "after having refined them and purified them as necessary." This fundamental "assimilation" that Congar was proposing would take specific form in other developments: "a policy of liturgical reform," which sooner or later, he foretold, would necessitate "new liturgical creations" and above all the "ecumenical movement."

We should remember that ever since the nineteenth century, the essential demand of liberal Catholicism had been coupled with a challenge to the authority of the Magisterium. The latter was, in practical terms, essential to the achievement of the former: if the Church and the modern world were to be reconciled, it was essential to relativize the anti-modern Magisterium. That is why we must not forget that the conclusion that the anti-infallibilists drew in 1870 was that *Quanta Cura* and the *Syllabus* had to be prevented from becoming dogma; nor should we forget that the lever that modernism used to obtain its wishes was the relativizing interpretation of dogma. The specific contribution of the 1950s was this: the question of the authority of the Magisterium, which had to be resolved if the liberals were to release the bolts with which the unyielding anti-modernism of the Roman texts had blocked their progress," was resolved by the concept of *dépassement* or "going beyond." Congar summed up this "going beyond" in his *Vraie et fausse réforme dans l'Église* with the phrase "the primacy of the pastoral." This method had two particular features: the first was, as Congar explained throughout his programmatic work, carefully to avoid touching "structures," that is to say, dogmas, thus avoiding the unfortunate outcome encountered by Luther following his "false reform of the Church"; the second was to aim at a reform of the actual ways in which the Church's faith and worship were expressed.

Changing the way in which the faith is expressed without affecting dogma seems *a priori* incoherent in the case of the Catholic economy, unless we uncouple the two terms, that is to say, we set the dogmatic mode of speaking aside in order to express the faith. The key to a "true reform" was therefore no longer the "faith without dogma" of the modernists, but a non-dogmatic expression of the faith. Doubtless there was nothing really original in that, since what it amounted to was a new form of the relativization of the Church's dogmas. But it did have this particular feature, this inspired touch, as one must admit, that it was positive in the technical sense of the word: it allowed the development of a new norm in the expression of the faith that "went beyond" or sidelined the previous norm, and therefore rendered unnecessary any attempt to demonstrate a rigorous coherence between the two norms, since the new term (a "pastoral" orthopraxy) had been developed in order to avoid any comparison with the old (dogmatic orthodoxy).

The first application that Congar made of this new "priority of the pastoral" was to develop an outline ecumenical program. He thus isolated the dogmatic difficulty (return or non-return of separated Christians to the Catholic Church) by integrating contraries: the re-united Church would no longer strictly speaking be the Catholic Church, since it would mark a development relative to this Church considered in her current state, "and in this sense it would be a different Church," but this development would nevertheless be a development of the Catholic Church, "and in this sense, it would not be a different Church, a different ecclesial body from the Catholic Church."

That therefore is the form that a "true reform of the Church" would take. For example, the reformers would no longer criticize the traditional dogmatic formulations related to the identity of the Church, but from now on, they would deal with the very principle of a precise definition explaining the content of the faith on the subject of the identity of the Church—a "scholastic" definition, as they disparagingly called it—by "going beyond" it.

CHAPTER 4

The *Nouvelle Théologie* and the Networks of Resistance

WHEN YVES CONGAR formulated this principle of "going beyond" in the ecclesiological field, he was only taking up with his particular talent ideas that were floating around in the thought of the period. In particular he aligned himself with the theologians forming what is called the *nouvelle théologie*, to use a term employed by Pius XII. From this group of thinkers, comprised of prominent Jesuits, there emanated a criticism of the traditional scholastic theology, which had exposed itself to criticism through a certain sclerosis, particularly in the version of scholasticism taught in seminaries. But beyond scholasticism, the target was the "rigidity" of dogmatic formulations, themselves largely dependent on this scholastic theology.

Once the hesitations that followed the modernist crisis had passed, twentieth-century Catholic intellectuals largely adopted the principle of historical criticism, just as in the sixteenth century, they had rediscovered "positive" theology, that is to say a theology directly founded on the study of the Fathers, or professing as much, and monastic theology, particularly that of Saint Bernard, which was less rigorously expressed than Thomist theology. When people spoke of rediscovery, they were in reality taking pleasure in setting both theologies against the scholastic method, while complacently disparaging it as narrow and outdated, with its *disputationes* (discussions) consisting of manuals divided up into questions, objections, and replies. The supporters of scholasticism certainly knew how to defend themselves: "It is exciting," wrote Dom Ghislain Lafont, "to see how a patristic expression, richly and concretely phrased, but often vivid and inexact, transforms into a scholastic expression, in which the right word expresses the exact meaning and hits the target in a much more real way, since it is closer to the truth."[1]

But the movement in favor of a return to positive theology had the wind in its sails. It asserted loudly that it was founded on the study of the Fathers of the Church, which had never been really abandoned, but to whom educated clerics, to tell the truth, now had easier access through specialist studies and more careful editions, published in the series *Sources chrétiennes* by Jean Daniélou, Henri de Lubac, and Claude Mondésert. The movement was therefore a complex one, which combined a current of ecclesiastical fashion with an undeniable advance in scholarship, and also with a project that was subversive of classical theology.

We must of course also mention Father Marie-Dominique Chenu, Regent of Studies at the Dominican study house at Saulchoir since 1932, whose book, *Une École de théologie, le Saulchoir*, was seen as a manifesto and was privately printed in same year as Congar's *Chrétiens désunis* appeared.[2] The book was put on the Index in 1942, and Chenu was relieved of his responsibilities, but it bore fruit after the War, when Chenu and Congar became figures emblematic of the renewal. *Une École de théologie* argued that the texts of the great scholastic authors, and notably those of Saint Thomas, should be considered in their historical context, a project in itself full of interest. But the application of historical criticism became criticism of the scholastic method itself. "The most perfect theological systematization," he wrote, "does not add an ounce of

---

1 "Théologie Mediévale," in *Témoignages*, Cahiers de la Pierre-qui-Vire, January 1952.

2 Marie-Dominique Chenu, *Une école de théologie: Le Saulchoir* (Tournai: Casterman, 1937); reprinted, ed. G. Alberigo, and others, preface by Réne Rémond (Paris: Cerf, 1985).

light and truth to the Gospel."[3] That of course was true in a certain sense: the New Testament contains the full plenitude of Revelation, and nothing could add to it. But from another point of view, the systematization that the theologians achieved is an approach that facilitates comprehension by human thought, itself rational by nature. Furthermore, the texts of the New Testament already contain a "systematization," to which the Gospel according to Saint John and the Epistles of Saint Paul, among other texts, bear witness. In reality, Chenu's criticism of a rational system—that is to say, his criticism of a Thomism that was less audacious than his own system, that of the Roman universities of his day—necessarily took as its basis a second rational system, his own. Because, taken at face value, Chenu's critical and scientific approach, like a snake devouring its tail, would have ended up in an anti-intellectual position.

The same could be said of the home of the *nouvelle théologie*, which was that of the French Jesuits, and in particular their study house at Lyon-Fourvière. We talk generally of the theological circle of Fourvière, but this is, to tell the truth, no more than a convenient localization, since Henri de Lubac lived at Fourvière, certainly, but taught at the *Institut Catholique de Lyon*, and Jean Daniélou and Gaston Fessard were Parisians. In 1946–48 a controversy put this theology under the spotlight. It was set in motion by the May 1946 issue of *Revue thomiste*, a publication edited by the Dominicans of Saint-Maximin. The issue contained an article by Father Michel Labourdette aimed at the Jesuits of Fourvière and Paris, and a critical review by Father Marie-Joseph Nicolas of a work of de Lubac.[4] The *Revue thomiste* attacked the disparagement of scholastic

---

[3] Jacques Duquesne, *Jacques Duquesne interroge le Père Chenu: un théologien en liberté* (Paris: le Centurion, 1975), 128.

[4] Michel Labourdette, "La théologie et ses sources," in *Revue thomiste*, 46 (1946), 353–71; Marie-Joseph Nicolas, Review of *Corpus Mysticum* by Henri De Lubac, ibid., 383–88.

theology by de Lubac, Daniélou, Fessard, Bouillard, and von Balthasar. In opposition to their *nouvelle théologie* the *Revue thomiste* upheld the application of the scientific and rigorous expression of Christian thought to the truths of the faith, and the objectivity of this work, that is to say, the possibility that the intellect can grasp, at least in its most certain outlines, a reality outside of time.

But the attack launched by the *Revue thomiste*, which was in fact quite diffident, even in the judgment of Father Raymond-Léopold Bruckberger, the journal's director, gave way under the Jesuits' contemptuous reply in *Recherches de science religieuse.*[5] Drawn up essentially by de Lubac, the reply's tone of a contemptuous refusal to engage displeased Chenu himself, who spoke of a "dismissal in perpetuity without right of appeal" (Étienne Fouilloux).[6] The truth was that the "attackers" of the *Revue thomiste*, trained by Maritain and supported by Abbé Charles Journet, at that time professor at the senior seminary of Fribourg in Switzerland, were paralyzed by a feeling of inferiority, so frightened were they of being identified with the "integrist" Thomism represented by Father Réginald Garrigou-Lagrange. The fact that they were really quite close to the Roman school of theology made them all the keener to distinguish themselves from it.

For at the same time Garrigou-Lagrange himself had gone on the offensive, but with much greater vigor, with an article entitled, "Where is the *nouvelle théologie* going?"[7] Intemperate though this attack may have seemed to his distinguished colleagues at Saint-Maximin,

---

[5] "La Théologie et ses Sources. Réponse aux Études critiques de la Revue Thomiste (mai–août 1946)," in *Recherches de science religieuse*, 33/4 (1946), 385–401.

[6] Étienne Fouilloux, "Dialogue théologique (1946–1948)" in Serge-Thomas Bonino, *Saint Thomas au XXe siècle. Actes du colloque du Centenaire de la Revue thomiste, 25–28 mars 1993* (Paris: Ed. Saint-Paul, 1994), 174.

[7] R. Garrigou-Lagrange, "La nouvelle théologie où va-t-elle?" *Angelicum*, 23 (1946), 126–45.

it penetratingly assigned the paternity of this *nouvelle théologie* to Maurice Blondel. The debt of Henri de Lubac (and of other Jesuits of his generation, such as Fathers Henri Bouillard and Yves de Montcheuil) to Blondel was well-known. Blondel, who was repelled by Thomism (and perhaps even more by Thomists), had proposed an apologetic that was fundamentally immanentist (i.e., holding that the desire for the supernatural was inscribed in the heart of every man) in order to cut the ground from under the feet of the modernists. It appeared that he had somehow opened up a third way between modernism and Thomism. He was the original starting-point of the adherents to the *nouvelle théologie*, and then later, after the Council, of the French group associated with the journal *Communio*. His influence on de Lubac explains the immanentist tendency of the thesis which de Lubac maintained in his book *Le surnaturel*: for de Lubac, the aspiration of each man for the supernatural infinite is located in the mind with which each man comes equipped.[8] This was a herald of the indistinct half-tones of the theologies of dialogue between religions and of the decree *Nostra Aetate*: was there not some supernatural yearning at the very heart, not just of the members of the non-Christian religions, but of the non-Christian religions themselves, viewed as religions?

It is then understandable that Pius XII should have dedicated a notable part of his encyclical *Humani Generis* to this theme, which had by then become classic: going beyond scholastic theology and dogmatic systematization. The encyclical was generally seen as aimed first at the school of Fourvière. The reader encountered in it a listing of the errors which could be called classic: relativism, a minimalist understanding of obedience, a

---

[8] Henri de Lubac, *Surnaturel: Études Historiques* (Paris: Aubier, 1946), English trans. by Rosemary Sheed, *The Mystery of the Supernatural* (New York: Herder and Herder; London: Geoffrey Chapman, 1967).

professed return to the sources. But this bringing together of analyses of the illness sounded a new note, at least in the common direction toward which the errors tended: certain theologians are neglecting the traditional magisterial definitions "with the idea of giving force to a certain vague notion"; "some want... to free dogma itself from terminology long established in the Church and from philosophical concepts held by Catholic teachers, to bring about a return in the explanation of Catholic doctrine to the way of speaking used in Holy Scripture and by the Fathers of the Church"; "the more they exalt the authority of God the Revealer, the more severely do they spurn the teaching office of the Church"; "it is clear how false is a procedure which would attempt to explain what is clear by means of what is obscure."[9]

Fifteen years separated the controversy between Saint-Maximin and Fourvière from the opening of the Second Vatican Council. Congar, Chenu, de Lubac, Daniélou, and many others, therefore had in their hands the key that would open the lock. Similarly, Paul VI's address during the Council's last General Meeting on December 7, 1965 came fifteen years after *Humani Generis*. The clash between traditional theology and great "intuitions" had already begun. Certainly, it is easy today to assume the role of the prophet and say that this was unavoidable, because of the theological debates that agitated the Catholicism of the 1950s. But was there another issue involved?

We could even identify, in the composite character of the revolutionary movement of the 1950s, the tensions that would come to the surface later within the conciliar majority, and the struggles of the post-conciliar period between those who were left in possession of the field. Thus, the *nouvelle théologie*, if it merits treatment as a well-defined movement, had complex links with what at the same period was called progressivism and its different

---

[9] Pius XII, Encyclical Letter *Humani Generis*, August 12, 1950, nos. 18, 14, 8, 21.

forms, the group *Jeunesse de l'Église*, led by Father Montuclard and forcibly dissolved in 1955, the *Union des Chrétiens Progressistes*, of André Mandouze, and *Économie et Humanisme*, of Father Louis-Joseph Lebret. They can be defined by their priority interest in mission to the working class, something which in some cases, through differing degrees of sympathy for the working class, became transformed into communism. Of course, the argumentative turmoil that surrounded the experience of the worker-priests, and that was sustained by publications such as *La Quinzaine* and *Témoignage chrétien*, in an atmosphere punctuated by the attempts of the hierarchy to restore discipline, created a sort of party spirit among all those who for one reason or another rejected the Roman line.

If therefore Chenu, who went into ecstasies over the purifying effect of the criticism of religion as the "opium of the people," could be classed among the progressivist thinkers, neither de Lubac, nor Daniélou, with whom the Regent of Studies at Saulchoir nevertheless had much in common, could be classed in that group. On the other hand, Congar, who was close to the worker-priests, but was interested above all in the structural transformation of the Church (turning the "Church-pyramid" upside down), in some way foreshadowed the reconversion that the progressivists would go through in the 1980s, after the collapse of Marxism, when they became an advanced liberal wing of Catholicism.

We should add that the priests and religious of the *nouvelle théologie* were closely linked to the liturgical movement: Fathers Pie Couturier and Marie-Alain Régamey, of the journal *L'Art Sacré*, already mentioned, or Fathers Aimon-Marie Roguet and Gustave Duployé, of the *Centre de Pastorale Liturgique* (CPL), all Dominicans, belonged to the same circles of thought as those at Saulchoir or the Jesuits of Fourvière. Ecumenism strengthened these links, as is shown by the case of Dom Lambert Beauduin, who was the founder of *Moines de l'Union*, at Amay-sur-Meuse and then at Chevetogne, in Belgium, with the journal *Irenikon* as its mouthpiece, but who was at the same time a member of CPL. Or again the case of Dom Olivier Rousseau, author of an *Histoire du mouvement liturgique* and collaborator with Dom Beauduin, closely linked with Daniélou and de Lubac, who after having edited the *Revue liturgique et monastique* took effective control of *Irenikon*, before playing an active role in the preparation of the conciliar texts on liturgy and ecumenism.[10]

The members of these circles of thought, active though they were in speaking and writing, were nevertheless just theologians. They were not yet the influences on the Magisterium that they would become at the Council. The more prominent among them had even incurred sanctions, which they would soon wear like the medals of a veteran: Chenu was dismissed from his responsibilities, Congar was transferred, while there were "purges" among the teaching staff at Fourvière. Nevertheless, the theological circles of which they were members were strongly rooted, carried along as they were on the wings of ecclesiastical conformism and the "course of history." Yet again, the transformation of majority opinion that was to occur at Vatican II was not written in the stars, but could matters really have evolved differently?

All the energy of *Ralliements* is directed toward conformism, which multiplies the pressure in a liberal direction and marginalizes the countervailing intellectual resistance, often leading to the break-up of that resistance. Garrigou-Lagrange's article had inspired Monsignor de Solages, rector of the *Institut Catholique de Toulouse*, to write a response that was mentioned repeatedly, commented on, and applauded, while the original article of Garrigou-Lagrange, consultor to the Holy Office and the most prominent Roman theologian of the period, was

---

[10] Dom Olivier Rousseau, *Histoire du mouvement liturgique: esquisse historique depuis le début du XIXe siècle jusqu'au Pontificat de Pie X* (Paris: Cerf, 1945).

looked on with embarrassed pity in the French Catholic faculties and treated with open contempt in convents and seminaries.[11]

Between the French participants Congar, Chenu, and the Jesuits of Fourvière on the one side, and the theologians on whom Pius XII depended on the other side, a real war had broken out over who was to be the doctrinal authority. In fact, the Romans only prepared themselves for the decisive engagement after the death of Pius XII in 1958. But what forces could they deploy on the ecclesiastical battlefield? On what strong points could they rely? In France, the Catholic integrists, heirs of Louis Veuillot and Cardinal Édouard Pie, were psychologically better prepared to sustain the combat than the timid Thomists of Saint-Maximin of Fribourg, but no longer had the requisite cultural footing or ecclesial base.

---

[11] Bruno de Solages, "Pour l'honneur de la théologie. Les contresens du R. P. Garrigou-Lagrange," *Bulletin de Littérature Ecclésiastique*, 48 (1947), 65–84.

CHAPTER 5

The Integrist Catholicism, to the Right of the Pope

DURING THE MID-1950s, Monsignor Gabriel-Marie Garrone, coadjutor of Cardinal Archbishop Jules-Géraud Saliège of Toulouse, had to explain himself before Cardinal Ottaviani: his critics charged him with certain statements in which they saw the influence of readings, in their view not fully understood, of German philosophers. We will understand nothing of the ecclesiastical world if we pass over the unquenchable grievances that grow within it, all—of course—for the greater glory of God. In 1969, less than fifteen years later, the roles were reversed: Garrone, now himself Archbishop of Toulouse, was part of the governing nucleus of the Curia of Paul VI, and used his influence to ensure that Alfredo Ottaviani, aged and now powerless, was forced by Paul VI to the equivalent of a retraction (Ottaviani had taken it upon himself, as we shall see, to make a virulent criticism of the new rite of the Mass). A journalist from Radio-Vatican asked Garrone, "Is what we have heard true, that the new rite represents the victory of an ecclesiastical party?" Cardinal Garrone, the new Prefect of the Congregation for Seminaries replied, "Not so much the victory of one party as the defeat of another."

Garrone's adversary, however, had not really bitten the dust, since Paul VI, because of this low thrust of the rapier, went on to modify slightly the presentation of the new missal. Then Monsignor Marcel Lefebvre took up the old cardinal's baton in rejecting the liturgical reform, with the result that the French cardinals who were Paul VI's close advisors, Jean Villot and Garrone, were left with a bitter and partial victory, and pushed Paul VI—whose psychological make-up was moreover very similar to theirs—in the direction of a complete refusal of any reconciliation with the integrists.

This partisan animosity is an element that we cannot ignore in the reformist fever of the French bishops who took part in the Council. So who were their integrist enemies? We need to go back to the nineteenth century to put them properly in context. The foundational event—in that it provoked a reaction—of what has been called Catholic integrism lies in the papal policy of *Ralliement*, even if we could quite naturally go back further to the *Syllabus*. The Toast of Algiers of Cardinal Charles-Martial Lavigerie, the lively debates that followed, and Leo XIII's *Au Milieu des Sollicitudes* created a new type of intransigent: papists opposed to the pope.[1] There had indeed already been signs foretelling the storm which was going to break out, such as the Pitra-Brouwers affair, in which Cardinal Jean-Baptiste Pitra, a Benedictine who had come from Solesmes, had quite overtly criticized the liberalism of Leo XIII and had been rapidly recalled to order.[2]

---

[1] On November 12, 1890, Cardinal Lavigerie, Archbishop of Algiers and Carthage, dining with officers of the French Mediterranean Fleet, proposed a toast to the French Navy. In the course of his speech he said that it was the first wish of the hierarchy that all Frenchmen should recognize and support the current political regime. Earlier that year, Leo XIII had given him the specific task of bringing French Catholics round to supporting the republican regime. The toast forced a choice on Catholic opponents of the republic, either to support the republic or to oppose the pope.

[2] In 1885 Leo XIII rebuked Des Houx, the intransigent editor of the *Journal de Rome*. Cardinal Jean-Baptiste Pitra, vice-dean of the Sacred College, expressed his support for Des Houx in a letter to Abbé Brouwers, a Dutch journalist, and was fiercely critical of the pope. In response, the pope published his reply to a letter of sympathy from Cardinal Guibert of Paris, and strongly rebuked all Catholics who presumed to interfere in the government of the Church. Cardinal Pitra, while not disavowing what he had written, was obliged to write a letter to the pope apologizing for the hurt that he had caused him.

These French Catholic integrists were heirs in a small way of the intransigents of the early nineteenth century, ultramontanes (supporters of the Roman liturgy, the moral teaching of Saint Alphonsus Liguori, the infallibility of the pope), violently hostile to the ideas of the Revolution and bourgeois society. They contained personalities as diverse as Philippe-Olympe Gerbet, Bishop of Perpignan; Dom Prosper Guéranger; Édouard Pie, Bishop of Poitiers, the most senior doctrinal representative of this party; and Charles-Émile Freppel, Bishop of Angers, the last great episcopal spokesman for the intransigent party before the call for *Ralliement*. We should add that not all the ultramontanes were intransigents, or were not so to the same degree, just as later we will find a certain number of anti-modernists among the bishops supporting the *Ralliement*, such as Abbé Hyppolyte Gayraud and Father Vincent Maumus: the growing success of ultramontanism was accompanied by great moderation, especially among the higher clergy, since it involved direct opposition to the principles of modern society.

So far as the opposite party is concerned—that of Charles de Montalembert; Félix Dupanloup; Marie-Dominique Sibour, Archbishop of Paris; and Henri Lacordaire—it was in general terms a product of Gallicanism. Again, the relationship of the conflict between liberals and intransigents to the conflict at the start of the century between Gallicans and ultramontanes is complex: Montalembert, the leader of the liberals, was a convinced ultramontane; Lamennais, the father of Catholic liberalism, with his anti-Gallicanism and his traditionalism, in the philosophical sense of the word, had inspired many of the intransigents (such as Gerbet and Guéranger), who had originally mostly been his followers.

The clear crystallization of the two parties occurred in 1864, when they divided for and against *Quanta Cura*, which condemned modern errors, and the *Syllabus*, which catalogued them. Pius XI and the nuncio, Raffaele Fornari, supported the intransigents in France, giving particular support to Veuillot's campaigns in *L'Univers*. But the position of the intransigents among the French clergy was nevertheless a weak one, and among the highest ranks they were in fact in the minority, notably because of the uncertainty of the French political world of the Second Empire. The final failure of the dynastic claims, from 1871 to 1877, definitively removed any direct political influence from the intransigents, and at the same time removed their need for any form of compromise with projects such as *Ordre Moral*.[3]

Rome also now found itself at a crossroads. The more the political regimes laicized themselves, the more difficult it became to reconcile the doctrinal principles of anti-modernism with the Roman policy of accommodation with the new regimes, sealed in France by the Concordat. French Catholics woke up one day to find themselves in a lay Republic, a pure—and soon a harsh—incarnation of this "novel conception of law" which Leo XIII condemned in his encyclicals with the utmost vigor.[4] The tension between daily life, on the

---

[3] The political situation in France, following defeat in the Franco-Prussian War in 1870 and the start of the Third Republic, was confused, with the Republican movement competing for power with monarchical parties supporting the claims of the Comte de Chambord or of the Comte de Paris. The new constitution of 1875 and the elections of 1877 marked the final eclipse of the monarchical parties. *Ordre Moral* was a monarchical movement, led by Albert duc de Broglie, *président du Conseil* in 1873–74.

[4] Leo XIII described the "novel conception of law," *ius novum*, as being based on the principles "that each [man] is so far his own master as to be in no sense under the rule of any other individual; that each is free to think on every subject just as he may choose, and to do whatever he may like to do; that no man has any right to rule over other men. In a society grounded upon such maxims all government is nothing more nor less than the will of the people, and the people, being under the power of itself alone, is alone its own ruler.... And since the people is declared to contain within itself the spring-head of all rights and of all power, it follows that the State does not consider itself bound by any kind of duty toward God" (Encyclical Letter *Immortale Dei*, November 1, 1885, nos. 24–26).

one hand (the government of this Republic nominated the bishops and wrote the rules authorizing the opening of new places of worship), and the magisterial principles on the other hand became so strong that a breakdown at one level or another was inevitable: either the reality of Catholic life would strictly follow magisterial principles and the Church would become more violently opposed to the democracy—an armed peace, a more or less active intransigent resistance—or there would in fact be an officially recognized discontinuity between reality and the magisterial principles.

Leo XIII chose the second alternative. Generally we pay too little attention to the shock caused by the position taken up by the pope, when he declared à propos democracy according to the principles of Jean-Jacques Rousseau, that "civil power, considered as such, is from God, always from God."[5] The intransigents felt the ground being taken from under their feet. It was a jolt similar to—though certainly much less important than—that produced by the declaration of Vatican II on religious liberty, seventy years later with, in between, almost exactly at the halfway point, the complex, but in some ways comparable, event of the placing of *Action Française* on the Index in 1926, followed by measures forbidding recalcitrants who continued to read the journal from receiving the sacraments. Similar causes produce the same reactions, with the earlier reactions explaining and contributing to the opposing positions taken up later.

One small but very significant action shows the extent of the intransigents' disarray: the foundation of the *Association Notre-Dame de Nazareth*. In Paris, one of those most representative of the group who began to be called *Catholiques intégraux* or even integrists (though this term, strictly speaking, refers to members of the Spanish party, an element in the Carlist movement, led

---

[5] Leo XIII, Encyclical Letter *Au Milieu des Sollicitudes*, February 16, 1892, no. 18.

by Ramon Nocedal) was Father Charles Maignen, of the Congregation of the Brothers of Saint Vincent de Paul. Maignen was one of those most prominently involved in social works at the end of the nineteenth century. He was Chaplain-General of the *Association Catholique de la Jeunesse Française* founded by Albert de Mun and Robert de Roquefeuil in 1886, and the inspiration behind the *Oeuvre des Cercles* founded by his uncle Maurice Maignen, along with René de la Tour du Pin, and Albert de Mun. Charles Maignen became particularly well-known during the 1880s, by taking up a series of positions supporting the intervention of the State in the protection of workers. In addition, because he had been trained in the school of Maurice Maignen, his thinking was anti-liberal and clearly in line with the *Syllabus* (Maurice Maignen and his companions had in 1871 signed an "address to Pope Pius IX" in which they affirmed their undying loyalty to the teachings of the Church and based their actions on the principles contained in *Quanta Cura* and the *Syllabus*). Charles Maignen appeared therefore to be one of the leaders of the struggle against the conciliators, naturally following in this regard what Albert de Mun had said in his speech delivered at Chartres at the congress of the *Union des Oeuvres Ouvrières Catholiques* on September 8, 1878, "We are the irreconcilable counter-revolution."[6] In October 1891, between the "Toast of Algiers" and the appearance of the encyclical, Charles Maignen and his closest friends, Arthur Loth, Paul Vrignault, and Fathers Émile and Henri Hello, founded the short-lived *Association Notre-Dame de Nazareth*, a sort of anticipatory *Sapinière*,[7] which soon set itself the goal of creating a movement

---

6 Charles-Alexandre Geoffroy de Grandmaison (ed.), *Discours du Comte Albert le Mun Député de Morbihan*, vol. 1, *Questions Sociales* (Paris: Poussielgue frères, 1888), 291–305.

7 *La Sapinière* (the pine plantation) is the colloquial French name of the *Sodalitium Pianum*, or *Société Saint-Pie V*, a semi-secret society, founded in 1909 by Msgr Umberto Benigni, with the support of Pius X. The purpose of the society was to identify and report on

that might bring about the election of a pope less liberal than Leo XIII at the next conclave.

Charles Maignen was moreover linked doctrinally with the former pupils of the French Seminary in Rome, through a bulletin, *La Correspondance intime des anciens Élèves de Santa Chiara*, in which one could see reflected the debates which were agitating the ecclesiastical world: notably liberalism and the doctrinal value of *Au Milieu des Sollicitudes*, themes that Charles Maignen would take up and explore in greater depth in his *Nationalisme, catholicisme, Révolution*.[8] Nevertheless, this endeavor was never going to be more than ephemeral because of the lack of combative spirit among the other clergy involved. We will see this demonstrated later on in the attacks on the early development of modernism, found for example in his *Nouveau catholicisme et nouveau clergé*.[9]

We need to turn again to this characteristic concentration on the politico-doctrinal line of the pope. One consequence of the post-revolutionary situation, with the almost complete disappearance of states taking Christian principles as their authority, was to accentuate to an extreme degree the centralization of Catholicism and above all its psychological centralization. The cult of the current pope, such as we know it, began under Pius VI, even before the French Revolution, during his triumphal visit of 1782 to the Austria of Joseph II, as a reaction—we today might say an identitarian reaction—to the societal rejection of Catholicism that the Enlightenment and the appearance of enlightened despots had set in motion. This veneration reached a peak when Pius IX was deprived of the Papal States. From now on the character of Catholicism depended as never before on the pope, not only

modernist currents within the Catholic Church. It was dissolved in 1914, briefly revived in 1915, and permanently dissolved in 1921.

[8] Charles Maignen, *Nationalisme, catholicisme, Révolution* (Paris: V. Retaux), 1901.

[9] Maignen, *Nouveau catholicisme et nouveau clergé* (Paris: V. Retaux), 1902.

on his magisterial documents, which were thoroughly anti-modern, but also on the more or less firm way in which he dealt with states and bishops, and above all on the political line that he took.

Even the agnostic Charles Maurras himself, who would appeal from an "ill-informed" to a "better-informed pope," would be enveloped in this atmosphere of waiting for an answer from the pope alone. The result is that any attempt to establish a line of succession between the integrists and the Gallicans of the Ancien Régime who supported the Four Gallican Articles is no more than guesswork, since the integrists were substantially Roman . . . even though despite Rome.

We should not immediately dismiss with a patronizing smile the ambition which Charles Maignen's small circle of friends professed, of influencing the next pontifical election. The group of persons with influence in the Church, even at this date, was comparatively small, and inclined to become quite lively. It was moreover easy to make contact with them as a group if one used the French language, which for ecclesiastics had remained the universal language. Charles Maignen's leaflets and articles, which were clearly expressed, and abounded in incisive irony, were particularly well-suited to setting friends and enemies in motion, even at the highest levels of the hierarchy. We could cite *La Souveraineté du Peuple est une hérésie*, aimed in fact at the calls for *Ralliement* and replying to a pamphlet by the Dominican Father Élisée-Vincent Maumus which appeared the same year, which claimed to find a justification for the sovereignty of the people in the *Summa Theologica* of Saint Thomas Aquinas.[10] Monsignor Umberto Benigni, founder of the famous *Sapinière*, pursued the same line in the succeeding

[10] Maignen, *La Souveraineté du peuple est une hérésie, à propos d'une brochure du R. P. Maumus* (Paris: A. Roger et F. Chernoviz, 1892); Elisée-Vincent Maumus, *La République et la politique de l'Église. Le pouvoir, la loi, la liberté* (Paris: P. Lethielleux, 1892).

pontificate of Pius X, stirring up ecclesiastical opinion by publishing commentary in his *Correspondance de Rome*, and then in *Rome et le Monde*, French-language bulletins spread by friendly publications such as Abbé Paul Boulin's *La Vigie*, or Abbé Barbier's *Critique du libéralisme*, or by publicists such as Father Salvien of *La Bonne Presse*. The small print-run of these publications should not deceive us: one of the characteristics of French integrist publishing was that it always nourished passionate feelings of support or opposition, even among the great number of those who had only encountered it by report. All this agitation—the deplorably exaggerated denunciations kept up by the integrists, and the marginalization that their opponents imposed on them—was characteristic of a Church that was already caught up in a deepening crisis.

Integrist Catholicism was a strange thing: very solidly based doctrinally whenever it spoke about the public rights of the Church, but jejune in the extreme whenever it defended scriptural positions that would today be regarded as fundamentalist. Charles Maignen, Dom Jean-Martial Besse (a monk of Ligugé, who was an equally stalwart opponent of *Ralliement* and of modernism), the Jesuit Julien Fontaine, Abbé Paul Boulin, the former Jesuit Emmanuel Barbier, and many others as well, therefore created this quite particular situation comprising Catholics who, all the while basing themselves on a corpus of Roman documents of ever increasing importance condemning the leading principles of modern society, had nevertheless got the politics wrong, in this sense, that the majority of the clergy and the bishops, encouraged by the instructions from Rome, was adjusting itself to the "novel conception of law." The situation of the integrist Catholics did not change substantially under the succeeding pontificate of Pius X. Certainly, they were absolutely in agreement with the new direction imparted by Pius and his Secretary of State, Cardinal Rafael Merry del Val. It is now quite certain that Pius X and his counsellors

(Cardinals Gaetano de Lai and Louis Billot) listened to and supported men like Maignen and Benigni. But in order really to understand the atmosphere of the pontificate of Pius X, as Émile Poulat has written in *Intégrisme et catholicisme intégral*, we must grasp "the interaction of a strong will and a feeble authority, a will that was much stronger than it is often asserted to have been, and an authority that was much weaker than everyone believes."[11] Pius X, Cardinals Merry del Val and de Lai, and *a fortiori* Monsignor Benigni and his *Sodalitium Pianum*, felt that they were living in a fortress under siege.

At the end of 1914 Rome returned to the policy of Leo XIII. The inaugural encyclical, of Benedict XV, Pius X's successor, *Ad Beatissimi Apostolorum*, contained some unmistakable allusions:

> . . . let no private individual, whether in books or in the press, or in public speeches, take upon himself the position of an authoritative teacher in the Church.... It is, moreover, Our will that Catholics should abstain from certain appellations which have recently been brought into use to distinguish one group of Catholics from another... that they should be most closely united with their bishop and most loyal to him.[12]

The *Sodalitium Pianum*, which had been in abeyance since the death of Pius X, its protector and beneficiary, was consequently forced to dissolve itself in 1921.

Above all, on December 29, 1926, Pius XI, who had now succeeded Benedict XV, placed the journal *L'Action Française* on the Index, a sanction that Pius X had judged inopportune (he had ratified the decree on January 29, 1914, but had deferred its publication). As has often been

---

[11] Émile Poulat, *Intégrisme et catholicisme intégral: un réseau secret international antimoderniste, la Sapinière, 1909–1921* (Tournai: Casterman, 1969), 67.

[12] Benedict XV, Encyclical Letter *Ad Beatissimi Apostolorum*, November 1, 1914, nos. 22, 24, 28.

remarked, the integrist Catholics had a sufficient number of reservations about the "young positivist school" to be able to understand the doctrinal reasons—which were not made fully explicit—behind this condemnation, that is to say, the naturalist tendencies of the Maurrasian system.[13] They had only shown a limited amount of sympathy for this movement, and they would have preferred it to take its inspiration from the monarchy of Saint Louis rather than that of Louis XIV. But they found themselves alongside the royalists of *Action Française* in numerous campaigns and refused to take the side of their detractors when the decree was published. Among the laity, an entire strand of Catholic intellectuals influenced by the Thomism of Maritain and close to the Maurrasian movement, though with a varying number of reservations or distinctions (both before and after the condemnation), Jean de Fabrègues, Jean Daujat, Jean-Pierre Maxence, and Louis Salleron would always be conflicted when it came to the calls for *Ralliement*.

The ambiguity in their position all arose from this: Maurras's Catholic critics quite rightly took issue with the influence on his thought of the positivism of Auguste Comte, and the fact that he paid no attention to the supernatural order. But these critics were themselves dependent on a different type of naturalism, that of liberal Catholicism and its derivatives, which specifically relegates the supernatural to the private world of the individual. Every theological dispute is also a political

---

[13] Positivism is the name assigned to a philosophical system associated with the French philosopher Auguste Comte, which focused attention on observable (or positive) facts and distrusted discussion of more abstract issues. The philosopher Charles Maurras was attracted by positivism, and this led him to identify laws of history which pointed to the necessity for a Catholic, monarchical regime. Integrist Catholics often found themselves on the same side as the followers of Maurras in debates, but remained suspicious of the positivist roots of his ideas and so spoke dismissively of his supporters as "the young positivist school."

dispute, and that was more true of this dispute than of any other: there was a political aspect to the neo-Thomism of Maurras's Catholic defenders, such as the Dominican Father Thomas Pègues, or to the Suarezianism of the Jesuit Father Pedro Descoqs and of Father Charles Maignen, but there was an equally political element to the philosophical thought of Maurras's opponents, Lucien Laberthonnière and Maurice Blondel.[14]

Given the context, Catholic integrists of every strand of opinion could not but see the condemnation of *Action Française* as an unexpected gift for the democracy associated with Aristide Briand.[15] Additionally, the condemnation marked the start of a very bleak period for them. In Rome, Cardinal Louis Billot, one of the Catholic integrists closest to *Action Française*, had to resign his cardinalate in 1927. Historical investigations of *La Sapinière* by the Sulpician Father Fernand Mourret and by Louis Canet, Advisor for Religious Affairs at the Quai d'Orsay, which were intended to furnish material to condemn the integrists, added oil to the flames. In the same year, Henri le Floch, a member of the Congregation of the Holy Spirit and Superior of the French Seminary in Rome, had to resign, and the director of *La Croix*, Abbé Georges Bertoye, was replaced. These actions reflected the iron will of Pius XI, who encountered, as one must admit, equally tenacious opponents: Monsignor Pierre-Eugène-Alexandre Marty, Bishop of Montauban, still had not passed the news on to his diocesan priests one year after the condemnation of *Action Française*, and adopted a threatening attitude toward those of them who, in obedience to the pope, wanted to refuse the sacraments to readers of the royalist journal. He was invited to resign on several occasions, and was finally dismissed on his

[14] Suarezianism denotes teaching derived from the theologian Francisco Suárez (1548–1617).

[15] Aristide Briand was a principal promoter of the 1905 Law of Separation. He was subsequently eleven times *Président de Conseil.*

deathbed. Without doubt, the prelates who were the most recalcitrant, such as Monsignor Jean-Baptiste Penon, Bishop of Moulins, exiled in a monastery, Monsignor Ernest Ricard, Archbishop of Auch, and Monsignor Gabriel de Llobet, coadjutor of the Archbishop of Avignon, were all what one might call followers of Pius X, and were all linked to Catholic integrists.

Pius XI was succeeded by Pius XII in 1939, and the new pontificate changed the situation yet again: even though the internal political stance was much more nuanced than under Pius X, and notably so far as concerned the episcopal nominations, which were hardly different from those of Pius XI, nevertheless the representatives of an integrist Catholicism found that they were again shown a great deal of sympathy at the highest level. But this integrist Catholicism was considerably weakened and seemed at first sight almost lost in a larger conservative trend of reaction against the progressive currents of the 1950s. However, we can say that under Pius XII, and especially at the end of his pontificate, the influential personalities found in the chief offices of the Curia, especially Cardinals Alfredo Ottaviani and Giuseppe Pizzardo at the Holy Office, along with an important group of teachers at Roman universities, or in other words those who wielded power over doctrine and at the center, were all on the same wavelength as the integrist Catholics.

These integrist Catholics, who had for the most part studied at Rome between the wars—such as Abbé Luc Lefèvre, founder of *La Pensée Catholique*, Abbé Victor-Alain Berto, who would be Monsignor Marcel Lefebvre's theologian at the Council, Abbé Alphonse Roul, Abbé Raymond Dulac, and Father Marcellin Fillère and Abbé André Richard, both founders of *L'Homme Nouveau*—were kept away from positions of responsibility, and in particular from the episcopate, to which ecclesiastics with similar qualifications were appointed without difficulty. Abbé Marcel Lefebvre owed his miter to the fact that he had entered the Congregation of the Holy Ghost, which at the time contained a large number of missionaries, at the prompting of his brother, one of the Fathers of the Congregation. Previously he had exercised the function of vicar in a parish of the diocese of Lille, and could expect at most a career as a professor in a seminary. Clearly, there was a relation of cause and effect between this marginalization of Catholic integrism and the fact that, following the Billot generation, the integrist ranks lacked sufficient individuals of a certain depth of character and intellect. Seen from France, the situation was quite paradoxical: the picture was one of comparatively obscure ecclesiastics and eccentric journals whose thought was nevertheless closer to the attitudes of the Roman circle that we have described, which was solidly established in the papal institutes and the Congregations, and which formed and reflected the papal Magisterium.

The phrase "the Roman School of Theology," which we have used several times, can seem rather vague. It is however a better description than anything else to the extent that the school's representatives were all products of papal universities and Roman ecclesiastical institutions or were members of their teaching staffs. The school included Dominicans, such as Réginald Garrigou-Lagrange, Marie-Rosaire Gagnebet, Luigi Ciappi, who from 1955 was Master of the Sacred Palace (the "pope's theologian") and would be raised to the cardinalate by Paul VI; Jesuits, such as Franz Hürth, a moral theologian, Sébastien Tromp, the closest of them to the thought of Pius XII, a protégé of Cardinal Tardini, and later Cardinal Ottaviani's right arm during the preparation for the Council; Franciscans, such as Ermenegildo Lio, the young Father Umberto Betti, who specialized in magisterial questions and was the School's final representative, since he was Rector of the Lateran University from 1991 to 1995; the philosopher Cornelio Fabro, a religious belonging to the Congregation of the Sacred Stigmata; Philip de la

Trinité, a Carmelite; and secular priests from Rome or who had come to Rome, like Monsignor Pietro Parente, an Assessor of the Holy Office, Monsignor Pietro Palazzini, Monsignor Dino Staffa, and Monsignor Antonio Piolanti, Rector of the Lateran University and editor of the journal *Divinitas*, which was above all the mouthpiece of the Roman school of theology. Monsignor Piolanti's career would have taken him to the highest levels if things had evolved differently and if the accession to the papacy of his nemesis Giovanni Battista Montini had not blocked his progress.

From this rather nebulous group, which lacked neither flexibility (Betti would quite definitely distance himself from Ottaviani's line during the Council, while Parente would depart from it on the question of collegiality), nor personal animosities, nor struggles for influence (such as that between Tromp, a professor at the Gregorian University, and Piolanti, of the Lateran University, for example), there emerged prelates like Cardinals Alfredo Ottaviani, Ernesto Ruffini, Giuseppe Siri, and Giuseppe Pizzardo. It was Parente who, with an article entitled *Nuove tendenze teologiche*, inspired Pius XII to use the term *nouvelle théologie* to describe the opposite theological party.[16] All these Roman ecclesiastics were close to Catholic integrism, especially Ottaviani, the most prominent among them, author of a treatise on the public law of the Church, and the most competent specialist in the doctrinal field covering the relations between States and the Church.

If the French networks of the *nouvelle théologie* defined themselves by their latent opposition to *Humani Generis*, the Roman circle and its outposts took *Humani Generis* as their principal starting-point, just as their intransigent predecessors had taken *Quanta Cura*. It is significant that their preferred targets, notably in articles in *Divinitas*,

[16] Pietro Parente, "Nuove tendenze teologiche," in *L'Osservatore Romano*, February 9–10, 1942.

were not the most "advanced" theologians like Edward Schillebeeckx or Hans Küng, but rather the moderate innovators like Daniélou, de Lubac, and von Balthasar, who would in fact themselves become the inspiration behind the Magisterium. It is equally characteristic of them that their reactive attitude toward a theology whose essential mark was criticism of dogmatic conceptualization took the form of an appeal to the infallibility of the contested doctrines. They dreamed of canons followed by anathemas, in the manner of previous councils, concerning the spiritual maternity of the Virgin Mary, the doctrine of the ends of marriage, the official confirmation of Thomism as a way of conducting theology, the mystery of divine worship, the ecclesiology of the Mystical Body, Biblical inspiration, etc. Moreover, the more clearly the intentions of Pius XII's successor, John XXIII, became defined, the more utopian became the Roman school's demands.

When the conciliar tournament began, the Roman circle suffered an immediate and total disaster. This event, which unhorsed the curial and Italian cardinals, forcing them to take sides—either going into silence or joining an opposition of the reformist type—precipitated what remained of French integrist Catholicism into a new and harsh period of conflict. The situation was unprecedented, since the Second Vatican Council's declaration *Dignitatis Humanae* was of a quite different level of importance from Leo XIII's *Au Milieu des Sollicitudes*.

For all that, these Roman prelates and theologians, convinced that they shared the almost magic untouchability of the papal anti-modernist teaching, had accepted—even if they had not provoked it—the confrontation of the Council which proved fatal for them. They constantly referred to the great encyclicals of Pius XII, over whose composition they had been consulted, or in whose formulation they had participated: *Mystici Corporis* of June 29, 1943, on the Mystical Body and the Church; *Divino*

Afflante of September 30, 1943, on biblical interpretation; *Mediator Dei* of November 20, 1947, on the liturgy; and *Humani Generis* of August 12, 1950, on the theological errors of the time. Armed with this material, they managed, up to a certain point, the preparations for Vatican II. All this was in vain. We could say that until this point Rome had retained the doctrinal positions of the intransigents (represented by Roman theology), while progressively relaxing the political positions taken by the same intransigents (and maintained by Catholic integrists). After the death of Pius XII, it was the intransigents' doctrinal positions themselves, maintained by Roman theology, that Rome prepared to relax.

CHAPTER 6

The "Maginot Line" Curia

CARDINALS OTTAVIANI AND Ruffini were the first to talk to the future John XXIII, during the conclave of October 1958, about summoning a council. That makes it all the more likely that the idea of a council, first studied by Pius XI, had often been discussed in Rome and at the heart of the Italian hierarchy, ever since the arrival of Pius XII in 1939. Ruffini, who was Archbishop of Palermo and one of the leaders of the "right" wing, definitely recalled that in February 1948 he had urged Pius XII to summon an assembly of this type. Pius had set in motion an exploration of the project between 1948 and 1952, a period during which initial preparations reached a fairly advanced stage (preparatory commissions, collection of relevant materials) under the direction of the Holy Office. The letter that had been drafted to be sent to a worldwide sample of bishops indicated the tone of the project:

> The quagmire of dangerous errors, as well as the grave perils which menace the Church and society—which led to the summoning of the First Vatican Council eighty years ago—so far from diminishing, seem on the contrary to have gotten worse.[1]

In the end, Pius XII decided to halt the preparation for this immense assembly which appears to have frightened him (it was anticipated that some 3,000 bishops and theologians would come to Rome). But at the end of his

---

[1] *La Documentation Catholique*, vol. 64, no. 1485 (January 1, 1967), cols. 57–58.

papacy the anti-modernists continued to look with some favor on the idea, dreaming of making *Humani Generis* the subject of a council, much as *Quanta Cura* had in a sense been the subject of the First Vatican Council.

If the general tenor of the project was to put a brake on movement, this was the consequence of the rigorous conservatism of those around Pius XII, and more generally of the hardening of integrist thought. But we should avoid concluding that, just because the project's direction was conservative, it was backward-looking. In reality, just as the nineteenth-century supporters of the *Syllabus* were concerned for the conditions in which people lived, so the early twentieth-century integrists, with Pius X and Merry del Val at their head, were reformers in the classic sense: that is to say that they were animated, as their Tridentine predecessors had been, by ideas of anti-modern reform embodying rigor, spiritual demands, and discipline. Something of that flavor could be found in the strange movement "For a better world" of the Jesuit Father Riccardo Lombardi, who remained unknown in France although he met with great success in Italy under Pius XII. He was an ardent supporter of conciliarism. The book that he published when the calling of Vatican II was announced, *Concilio, per una riforma nella carità*, could have suited reformers of the left as well as of the right.[2] There was something of Savonarola's enthusiasm in this popular preacher, who urged bishops to undertake "a new Tridentine reform," and who wanted especially to reform and purify the Curia by making it "return to the Gospel." John XXIII, who had difficulty in appreciating Lombardi's critical and pessimistic style (unlike Paul VI, who was quite romantic and liked him a lot), ended up by ceasing to support him.

To this current, moreover, there corresponded one of the parties arising from the liturgical movement, which

[2] Riccardo Lombardi, *Concilio, per una riforma nella carità* (Roma: Edizioni Apes, 1961).

we could call "restorationist" in contradistinction to the "progressivist" party, and which has been totally obscured by that party and is ignored almost completely by historians. This party was especially interested in the study of liturgical sources and was far from being hostile to a re-establishment of original "forms." It was principally based at the abbeys of Solesmes and Montserrat, and at the Pontifical Institute of Sacred Music in Rome, which was overseen by a leading musicologist, Monsignor Higinio Anglés Pamies. We can thus identify a counter-reform party at the heart of the liturgical initiatives preceding the Council, of which the central project was certainly the development and diffusion of Gregorian chant, but also the liturgical education of the faithful and their education through liturgy (liturgical catechesis), the liturgical apostolate in and through youth movements, etc. In short, this party could claim at least as much responsibility as the *Centre de Pastorale Liturgique* for the origins of the liturgical re-awakening, that is to say for the work of Dom Guéranger and the support given by Saint Pius X.

What then were the tactical errors committed at the first session of the Council, and who was responsible for losing the battle? The first reason for the defeat lies in a misunderstanding of the personality of Angelo Roncalli, who became John XXIII.

Roncalli's sympathies, his established relationships, the political positions that he had adopted, particularly his active support for the *popolari*, the Christian democrats of the day, his long-standing friendship with Giovanni Battista Montini, pro-Secretary of State and then Archbishop of Milan, who was considered a liberal and who would perhaps have become pope in 1958 if he had been a cardinal, his preference for optimism and an eirenic approach,[3] which went far beyond the mere requirements of civilized conduct, all meant that the determining

[3] An eirenic approach is one that seeks, wherever possible, a peaceful solution or means of proceeding.

principles of his pontificate were not as difficult to predict as was asserted, though their consequences were another matter. None of these factors excluded a very conservative sensibility, strictly speaking, that is to say one that only superficially matched that of the militant counter-reformers. As the nuncio in Paris, Roncalli had shown much opposition to the "new priests" of the *Mission de Paris* or the *Mission de France*, so dear to Cardinal Suhard, he was indignant when people spoke favorably to him of Teilhard de Chardin, and he was not uninvolved in the decision to keep de Chardin at a distance.

Was there really a "mystery of John XXIII," as historians often say, as they ask themselves how this prelate with no strong distinguishing features, whom one would have hesitated to class as liberal or conservative, was able to become the pope of Vatican II? If there is a mystery, it resides simply in this: if we imagine that Angelo Roncalli had not been elected pope and that someone else had summoned the Council, the Patriarch of Venice would have been part of the vast majority of bishops who took part in the course of events without any great difficulty, doubtless with some reservations over secondary issues, but basically committed, as being something that was entirely natural, to the essentials of the Church's change of direction. It just happens that this bishop, who was completely suited to following the process, was the one who set it in motion.

So it was that at the 1958 conclave, the electors came to support Roncalli, but only at the eleventh vote, at the end of an election that had not been easy. Roncalli had pursued quite an effective campaign among his fifty-two colleagues, presenting himself as the candidate for a transition, a transition between two epochs and between two opposed currents of thought. His age—seventy seven years—allowed the reformers to envisage a short pontificate at the end of which Montini would have every chance of succeeding him. Montini himself, a joint pro-Secretary of State with Tardini (Pius XII had decided not to nominate a Secretary of State following the death of Cardinal Luigi Maglione in 1944), had been kept away from Rome, without being nominated cardinal, under pressure from cardinals on the right of the Curia, Giuseppe Pizzardo, Alfredo Ottaviani, Nicola Canali, and Clemente Micara. Roncalli's character moreover was not such as to cause concerns for the right wing, who had suffered also from the inaccessibility of Pius XII, who had adopted an almost Olympian detachment, isolating himself all the while behind domestic concerns. The curial right, well entrenched in the congregations, thought that it would have greater freedom of action under a pontiff who was less authoritarian and easier to control. This moreover is how things turned out. One example: *L'Osservatore Romano* adopted the practice of smoothing over the inappropriate or unwise comments that "good Pope John" inadvertently made during his impromptu addresses, a condescending liberty that would have been unimaginable under Pius XII. After a pope of great eminence, a "decent type" was now raised to the throne of Peter, good-natured, affable, who encouraged his interlocutors to speak freely. To be honest, the votes of the right wing were split between Roncalli, who had also secured the support of the French cardinals, Pietro Agagianian, and Aloisi Masella, Tardini's candidate. The determining factor which ultimately led the votes of the right to coalesce around Roncalli seems to have been the implicit assurance that he gave that he would not recall Montini to the post of Secretary of State, that is to say, Prime Minister of the Holy See, and that he would nominate Tardini as Secretary of State.

Once Roncalli had been elected, the second big mistake of the curial right wing was to participate in the launching of a process of reformation that it could not control. Whatever was the tenor of discussions on this subject within the conclave between Ruffini, Ottaviani, and Roncalli, it remains true that the inspiration behind the Council was that of John XXIII, warmly approved by Tardini, the first to be officially informed. The supposed "glacial silence" with which the cardinals, assembled in the Basilica of Saint Paul Outside the Walls, received the news from the mouth of the pope is a tendentious legend: on an occasion of this sort, which was comparable to the announcement of a promotion to the cardinalate, protocol did not allow for a response by the cardinals. In fact, John XXIII's expectations from the Council were quite vague, although definitely different from those of the Secretary of State: in John XXIII's mind, the invitation extended to the Protestants and the Orthodox to unite with the Catholic Church played a greater role, at any rate to begin with, than the idea of a reform that would bring the Church up-to-date, an *aggiornamento.* The Church would show her true nature to the world by means of this magnificent reunion. He pictured to himself these solemn ceremonies, deriving their popularity from their splendor, something that appealed to him much more than it would have done to the ascetic Pius XII. So far as concerns the *aggiornamento*, apart from the fact that it would facilitate unity with the separated brethren, something which gave it a certain focus, it was still difficult to say to what it would amount. Congar remained full of worries up until the opening of the Council, as his private journal reveals.

From the announcement of the Council, on January 15, 1959, at Saint Paul Outside the Walls, to the opening of the assembly, on October 11, 1962, there was every kind of maneuvering. The party supporting "movement" found itself bogged down in the wide-ranging program, which comprised the "adaptation of Church discipline to the needs and conditions of our times."[4] This party therefore started openly to denounce the Ancien Régime. For example, in his programmatic book on the Council, reform, and reunion, Abbé Hans Küng, a young

[4] John XXIII, Encyclical Letter *Ad Petri Cathedram*, June 29, 1959.

theologian from German-speaking Switzerland, who was nominated to the Council as an expert in 1962,[5] described the Holy Office explicitly as the "Bastille." The book had a preface written by Cardinals Achille Liénart of Lille and Franz König of Vienna. At the same time, the creation of a Secretariat for Christian Unity, suggested by Cardinal Augustin Bea, to whom it fell to lead the secretariat, proved to be a considerable advantage for this party. The theme of ecumenism allowed theologians regarded as suspect under Pius XII to lead opinion, and particularly that of the Supreme Pontiff, who additionally involved a certain number of them (Congar and de Lubac, for example, but also Chenu) in the preparatory work as consultors. It is noticeable that between 1959 and 1962 John XXIII's tone changed considerably. In his first encyclical, *Grata Recordatio*, clearly inspired by the circle around Ottaviani, he denounced "certain schools of thought and philosophy and certain attitudes toward the practical conduct of life which cannot possibly be reconciled with the teachings of Christianity."[6] In the opening speech of the Council, *Gaudet Mater Ecclesia*, of October 11, 1962, it was precisely that condemnatory line of thought at which he took aim when he launched his famous attack on "prophets of doom who announce sinister portents as if the end of the world were coming."[7]

At the same time there occurred a phenomenon not unlike the "reaction of the nobles" in France, during the reign of Louis XVI, in the years that preceded the Revolution.[8] There was the same impression of successive lurches to the right, emanating from the Curia,

[5] Hans Küng, *Konzil und Wiedervereinigung; Erneuerung als Ruf in die Einheit* (Vienna: Herder, 1960); English trans. by Cecily Hastings, *The Council and Reunion* (London: Sheed and Ward, 1961).

[6] John XXIII, Encyclical Letter *Grata Recordatio*, September 26, 1959, no. 17.

[7] *Gaudet Mater Ecclesia*, no. 4.

[8] In the years preceding the Revolution, opposition from some nobles to reforms which might undermine their position had the unintended effect of hastening the Revolution.

none of which had any effect, with the result that the tendency that they wished to neutralize only seemed all the more irresistible.

Ottaviani, who headed the Supreme Sacred Congregation of the Holy Office, a "super-ministry" among the Vatican congregations, appeared endowed with such authority that in Roman circles there circulated the adage, "Tardini rules, Ottaviani governs, and John blesses." But the authority of the Holy Office was, in fact, of variable strength. Thus, for example, in a *monitum* of June 30, 1962, following an examination of the works of Father Teilhard de Chardin set in motion by Monsignor Parente, Assessor at the Holy Office, de Chardin was warned against the errors that his works had supported, which were "so serious that they are offensive to Catholic teaching."[9] Far from fading away, the fashion for de Chardin's thinking, in the years following the *monitum*, found a success among the clergy and in the seminaries that is astonishing today, when no one any longer takes the theories of the visionary Jesuit as authoritative.

Cardinal Giuseppe Pizzardo, for example, Secretary of the Holy Office from 1951 to 1959, and also, from 1939, Prefect of the Congregation for Seminaries, a relic of the concentration of offices at the end of the reign of Pius XII, informed the French bishops in July 1959 that they should call a complete halt to the experiment of worker-priests. This definitive decision was withdrawn six years later. The truth is that the Curia never succeeded in getting it fully enforced by the French bishops. We must admit, however, that the decision to interrupt the experiment of worker-priests was taken not under Pius XII but under John XXIII.

The authority of the law continued to crumble. A document that was almost unenforceable, which should be seen in the context of the pre-conciliar discussions on the

---

[9] *Acta Apostolicae Sedis* [Official Acts of the Holy See] LIV (1962), 526.

language of the liturgy, was from this point of view most ill-advised: the apostolic constitution *Veterum Sapientia* of February 22, 1962, of which John XXIII pronounced himself fully supportive but which he completely failed to defend. Drawn up by Cardinal Antonio Bacci, who spoke Latin as if it were his mother tongue, and who supported Ottaviani without fail throughout the Council, it required Latin to be used again in teaching in seminaries, a requirement whose unenforceability was only matched by the solemnity of its approach, at least in France.

Cardinal Giuseppe Siri, Archbishop of Genoa, regarded as the "dauphin" of Pius XII but who was too young in 1958 to be elected pope, and who very effectively led the Italian Episcopal Conference, tried for his part to devote all his influence to blocking the policy of the opening to the left set in motion in 1960 by the Christian Democrat leader, Aldo Moro. But at the same time, John XXIII was receiving first Amintore Fanfani and then Moro and assuring them that the Church did not wish to interfere in political issues, thus inspiring the typically Roman dismissive comment, "Siri wanted to send Moro to hell, but has got himself sent to Limbo!"[10]

It was becoming clearer and clearer that the orthodox Roman party was not, despite all its efforts, the party favored by the pope. The party was all the weaker, in that it was an attitude rather than even a very lightly organized grouping. For example, right at the beginning of the Council, we saw Cardinals Ruffini and Ottaviani showing a total lack of concerted action while publicly opposing each other on procedural questions. Even before the start of the debates, there was a visible lack of decisiveness which was deeply damaging to the cohesion and efficacity

---

[10] Amintore Fanfani was prominent on the left wing of the Christian Democrats, and was prime minister on six occasions from 1954 to 1987. Aldo Moro, a more centrist Christian Democrat, was prime minister five times from 1963 to 1976, but was murdered by the Italian Red Brigade in 1978.

of the party, whose members showed increasing concern even though they were still unaware that they in fact had their backs against the wall. Quite unlike Pius XII's project of a council supervised by the Holy Office, John XXIII's project comprised a double-headed operation. Tardini was coordinating the whole of the preparation, and in particular was steering the Central Preparatory Commission, which was presided over by the pope and was a council in miniature with about a hundred members. Ottaviani directed the Theological Commission, of which the secretary was Sébastien Tromp SJ, appointed as having been the principal drafter of *Mystici Corporis*. The Theological Commission included among its members and influential consultors Fathers Marie-Rosaire Gagnebet, Luigi Ciappi, Ermenegildo Lio, Umberto Betti, Philippe de la Trinité, Franz Hürth, Joachim Salaverri and Monsignor Antonio Piolanti. Cardinal Ottaviani had been forced to include in his Commission some consultors of the liberal party, such as Fathers Joseph Lécuyer, Henri de Lubac, and Yves Congar, whose influence nevertheless remained limited: Congar noted in his journal that he felt as if he had been taken hostage. This Commission was responsible for all questions relating to Revelation, the faith, and morals, but even though it had the right to inform itself, it did not exercise as close a supervisory role over the other Roman congregations on doctrinal matters as did the Holy Office. Though the president of the Theological Commission put up a resistance over the subject, it was the Central Preparatory Commission, clearly less homogenous in its composition, which had the last word in all matters. The Roman school had the advantage there, but it had to defend its ground in debates that were at times tense.

Typically, Cardinals Tardini and Ottaviani had neglected to prepare opinion in advance, unlike the Curia of Pius IX in advance of the First Vatican Council, something for which that Curia has often been reproached. The situation however was entirely different: the topic driving forward the earlier council was papal infallibility, which had the double advantage of being popular and of tending toward the consolidation of authority, while the topic behind Vatican II, that of the unity of Christians, was as vague as it was exposed to all sorts of demagogic "openings."

There was one point on which Tardini and Ottaviani were in complete agreement. They both wanted the council to be brief, as indeed was the hope of John XXIII, who thought that it might be over by Christmas 1962. Tardini occupied himself with channeling the pope's thoughts, all the while keeping an eye on the preparations for the assembly. When Tardini, a highly skilled politician, died on July 30, 1961, to be replaced by a slender personality, Amleto Cicognani, it was like a second death of Pius XII. Cicognani's death reduced the chances of the curial right further, but it is unlikely that he could have saved the structure that he had put in place and that collapsed under the first few blows inflicted by the conciliar majority.

Cracks never cease to get bigger. The cumbersome preparatory structure, which was sufficiently effective to put in place traditional schemata dealing with Tradition and Scripture or the Church,[11] despite the discordant voices of experts not yet sure of themselves, nevertheless included two elements animated by a rather different spirit: the Commission on the Liturgy and the Secretariat for Christian Unity.

Cardinal Arcadio Larraona, who presided over the Commission on the Liturgy from February 1962, inherited the schema *De Sacra Liturgia* which his predecessor, Cardinal Gaetano Cicognani, four days before his death,

---

[11] A schema (plural, schemata) is a preparatory draft. Before the Council assembled, the curia as usual produced preparatory drafts, or schemata, of all the documents that the Council was expected to publish.

had approved after much hesitation, thinking it to be deeply iconoclastic. Larraona did all that he could to bring the schema into order by frequent reference to the Central Commission, imposing, for example, a limit on concelebrations and pushing back against proposals to allow the laity Communion in the Chalice.[12] He also removed the secretary to the Commission, Father Annibale Bugnini, and made him withdraw from all teaching in the Roman universities, although it was Father Bugnini who would later be appointed secretary to the Commission appointed to implement *Sacrosanctum Concilium*. The Commission on the Liturgy was a real melting-pot. It contained highly active consultors who were in favor of important changes, like the Belgian Benedictine Dom Bernard Botte, and the Frenchmen Pierre-Marie Gy, Pierre Jounel, Antoine Chavasse, Aimon-Marie Roguet, and Aimé-Georges Martimort, who was one of the firmest supporters of concelebration (to a maximum of eighty concelebrants…) facing *ad populum*. The most significant differences arose over the subject of the possible translation of parts of the Mass itself: Latin was defended by Monsignor Anglés Pamies, and the vernacular languages by the Benedictine Cipriano Bagaggini, who had been excluded from the Theological Commission because of his movement in the direction of the left. This was the context in which *Veterum Sapientia* was promulgated.

Despite all this, it is not possible to say that the proposals of the Commission on the Liturgy were explicitly revolutionary. Outside the Commission moreover, in general terms, the right was supportive of substantial reforms: the former archbishop of Dakar, Monsignor Lefebvre, a member of the Central Commission, was openly supportive of the introduction of the vernacular

---

[12] The original texts of this and other schemata are published in *Acta et Documenta Concilio Oecumenico Vaticano II Apparando. Series II (Praeparatoria)*, vol. III, parts I and II (Rome: Typis Vaticanis Polyglottis, 1969).

languages into certain parts of the ritual of the sacraments. In reality, the liturgy, being in certain respects a manifestation of the Church's doctrine, has a great capacity to reflect the state of the profession of Faith. Certainly, the majority of the experts were close to avant-garde European theologians, and were particularly attuned to the ecumenical spirit, but no clear direction of change had yet been decided on. As was entirely natural, it would be the role of liturgical questions to reveal what the Council was teaching as doctrine: if the Council had evolved as Tardini intended, there could have been, from the liturgical point of view, a clearer breakthrough in a conservative direction, with a continuation of reforms of the type that Pius XII had undertaken; alternatively, and this is what actually happened, the reforms could reflect, through a general refashioning of worship, the ecclesiological transformation established by the doctrinal texts. What is true throughout is that the importance of the party of movement at the heart of the Commission was a symptom of the position in which doctrine now found itself.

It was in Cardinal Bea's Secretariat for Christian Unity, which contained Monsignor Johannes Willebrands, Father Gustave Thils, Monsignor Émile De Smedt, Father Jérôme Hamer, and Monsignor François Charrière, that the most burning questions were debated. Apart from that of the relationship of the Church and the People of Israel, which the office of the Secretary of State withdrew, the discussions concentrated on two points which would determine the direction taken by the Council: the definition of ecumenism, and the abandonment of the doctrine of tolerance in favor of the doctrine of religious liberty.

The first point was a matter of ecclesiological order and would encroach on the domain of magisterial activity itself. What the specialists in ecumenism had to do was to define ecumenism in theological terms. Their intention was to do this in line with the idea formalized by Congar, that is to say by explaining that the ecumenical movement was of a different nature from individual or collective conversion, without denying that the Catholic Church was the true Church. And entirely naturally, in order to square this particular theological circle, they also made use of an idea that was circulating in the thought of the times (and in the pages of *Vraie et fausse réforme*), that of a Magisterium that was "simply pastoral." Little by little, therefore, the sub-commission tasked with preparing a doctrinal proposition drew the conclusion that this was not the right moment to draw up a rigorously doctrinal text. In the end, they even abandoned the following apparent definition, whose involuntary humor seems to have escaped the drafters: "By ecumenism, we understand all the efforts that are being contemplated to realize ecumenicity." The proposed conciliar text that reached the Central Commission therefore invited the Church to engage in the ecumenical project, an unprecedented doctrinal adventure, without its nature being defined. This was a remarkable "godsend," which would prove a formidable detonator, capable of exploding the entire doctrinal and disciplinary structure.

The Council was therefore, without realizing it, on the road toward a new method of expressing the faith, no longer dogmatic, but in some way para-dogmatic. We really need to appreciate the extraordinary manner of this method of proceeding: preparations were being made to propose to the organs of the Magisterium, the pope and the bishops, that they should renounce any attempt to fulfil their function at the moment which would have been most suitable for them to fulfil it, namely the holding of a general council. A doctrinal issue was going to be placed on the agenda, but instead of either making a positive decision, that is to say a dogmatic decision, or refusing to make a decision for the moment and leaving theologians free to discuss the matter, what would be officially adopted was a sort of semi-dogma, a pastoral line with the implications for the faith left indeterminate.

The process is even better understood if we think of the mathematical process of "approximating a limit" which can be applied to the doctrine of religious liberty. Ecumenism, the dialogue with religions, was going to come up against the earlier doctrine of expediency, so to speak. So far as concerns religious liberty, it was not possible to avoid the sharp edge of earlier formulations: anything said differently would necessarily contradict those formulations. The problem of religious liberty was the second point on which discussion in the Secretariat for Christian Unity focused. It was so important that it was detached, during the Council, from the decree on ecumenism to become the subject of a major text of Vatican II, the declaration *Dignitatis Humanae*. In reality, the question of religious liberty naturally interlocked with that of ecumenism: the Church wanted to cease giving an impression of Machiavellianism in its dealings with non-Catholics, appealing to religious liberty when Catholics were in a minority, and merely tolerating other religions when Catholics formed a majority within a nation. The secretary of the WCC, Willem Visser 't Hooft, had moreover, with an eye to the preparation of the Council, expressly asked the Catholic Church to change its doctrine on this subject. More generally, ecumenism was closely connected to the project of bringing the Church "up-to-date": if she wanted to show herself in a new light, she absolutely had to recognize the value that the modern world accords to the peaceful co-existence of different opinions.

A sub-commission, presided over by Monsignor François Charrière, Bishop of Fribourg in Switzerland, prepared a text. It is striking that it was this same Monsignor Charrière who later accorded juridical status to the fraternity led by Monsignor Marcel Lefebvre, the best-known opponent of religious liberty. The result was that the members of the sub-commission agreed on December 27, 1960, on what has been called the *Fribourg Document*, the first draft of what would become the conciliar declaration. This project received very many modifications until it was adopted five years later, on the December 7, 1965. Nevertheless, we should note that from the *Fribourg Document* onward, the traditional doctrine was set aside: the document replaced the doctrine of the possible tolerance of error with that of the right to liberty. Certainly, the text still avoided the word "liberty," but it used the word "tolerance" while giving it, as the authors said, a positive value, in the sense that moral theologians give to the word, that is with the force of a "right."

In theory, the document on religious liberty should have been presented to Ottaviani's Theological Commission. Ottaviani, who was the intellectual successor of Taparelli d'Azeglio, the principal authority for Leo XIII and Pius XII in the area of the public law of the Church, was by that very fact the most competent opponent of religious liberty. Cardinal Bea obtained from John XXIII, in an audience on February 1, 1962, the decision that the foreseeable opposition of the Theological Commission should be bypassed, and that both this document and the document on the dialogue with the Jews should be presented directly to the Central Commission. The episode is not in itself of great importance, but it is nevertheless extremely significant. The Theological Commission, like the Holy Office, acted in the name of the pope. John XXIII was therefore withdrawing a contentious document from the appropriate doctrinal oversight, effectively suspending his own magisterial judgment.

It was therefore before the Central Commission, in June 1962, that the confrontation between Bea and Ottaviani took place. A certain number of Ottaviani's supporters declared that Bea's document was unacceptable from the viewpoint of Catholic doctrine as it had been understood since the end of the eighteenth century. The Theological Commission had carefully put together its *De Ecclesia*, whose chapter 9 discussed "the relationship of the Church and the State and religious tolerance," in order to clarify the principles behind the issue of religious liberty, while re-iterating the well-established doctrine of tolerance. Ottaviani could have raised the stakes considerably, bringing in the term heresy, as the minority did when the project was being examined by the Council. But the pope had in effect given the green light, and the leader of the Holy Office, whose relationship with John XXIII had become less and less trusting, found himself confronted with a situation which was for him inconceivable: defending the faith despite the pope, not to say against the pope. Like the rest of the Roman school, he was convinced that the supreme Magisterium could not give up the fight. Ottaviani therefore temporized, on the assumption that the Magisterium would pronounce its verdict at the Council. He could not conceive of the possibility that the magisterial structure itself could be brought to a halt and that the exercise of its supreme teaching role could be relegated to a dusty attic. It was decided that in the three months remaining before the opening of the Council a mixed commission would be formed (comprising members of the Theological Commission and of the Secretariat for Christian Unity), but Ottaviani ensured that it never met. After all, what sort of compromise could it have reached?

This chapter of *De Ecclesia* thus forms a sort of boundary marker. It was the final statement, admittedly not official but prepared for official adoption, of the traditional doctrine on the most disputed point of the relationship between the Church and the modern world:

> The civil power cannot be indifferent toward religion. Since the civil power has been established by God to help men acquire a truly human perfection; it must not only offer its members the opportunity of procuring for themselves temporal goods, whether material or of a more cultural nature, but must also help

> them so that the spiritual goods may abound to enable them more easily to lead their human life in a religious way.... Also, in establishing laws the civil state must conform itself to the precepts of natural law...[13]

Everything therefore would be in play at the Council: either the chapter would be approved and it would invalidate the text on religious liberty, or the latter text would be approved and the teaching of the chapter would be rendered obsolete. We could say that each of the texts represented the leading edge of the two opposed projects for the Council that was about to open. What is more, if the Council had approved the Ottaviani text, the assembly would have made a pronouncement on a quite different doctrinal level from that which it did in fact adopt.

---

[13] *De Ecclesia*, 9. *Constitutionis dogmaticae Lumen gentium synopsis historica*, Vatican Council (2nd: 1962–1965: Basilica di San Pietro in Vaticano), ed. Giuseppe Alberigo and Franca Magistretti (Bologna: Istituto per le scienze religiose di Bologna, 1975), 308.

CHAPTER 7

October 1962

ONE OF THE most astonishing features of the history of Vatican II is that the liberal wing did not realize its strength and doubted whether it would be victorious. Its victory came to it as a complete surprise. It secured this victory in two stages: a breakthrough in the battle over procedure, and the rout of the curial right when the texts were examined.

The bastions which had to be demolished, to take up the metaphor of von Balthasar (Pope Francis later talked of walls to be levelled), were defended by Cardinal Alfredo Ottaviani, who had the title of Pro-Prefect of the Holy Office, rather than Prefect, because the Supreme Congregation, tasked with watching over doctrine, which was the pope's own very specific task, was nominally presided over by the pope. Ottaviani, a sixty-two-year-old Roman, the eleventh of the twelve children of a baker in the working-class district of Trastevere, had spent his entire career in the shadow of Saint Peter's Basilica, as much on the pastoral side (youth work) as in his curial functions, initially at the Secretariat of State, and then at the Holy Office. He was robust in character, forceful in speech, and of a strong physique, but was afflicted by a glandular swelling in his neck which progressively deformed his formerly classic profile of a Roman senator, and above all by an eye disease which gradually deprived him of his sight.

The success of the liberal wing, though they made up the majority, would never have happened without the support of John XXIII. He of course, as we all know, had opened the flood-gates when he opened the Council, in his famous address *Gaudet Mater Ecclesia*. Right at the start of play, he announced that Vatican II would be different from its two predecessor Councils, Trent and Vatican I, and would not be anti-modernist. Those looking for a council in continuity with *Humani Generis* should say to themselves, "In these modern times [the prophets of gloom] can see nothing but prevarication and ruin.... We feel we must disagree with those prophets of gloom, who are always forecasting disaster, as though the end of the world were at hand." That evening, the pope told his secretary, Monsignor Loris Francesco Capovilla, that during his address he kept glancing at Ottaviani, worried about how he would react. But the most significant statement would come in what followed: the Second Vatican Council, in contradistinction to all the previous councils, would neither dogmatize positively (in the form of canons) nor negatively (in the form of anathemata). From one point of view, it being taken for granted that all adhered to "the teaching of the Church in its entirety and preciseness, as it still shines forth in the Acts of the Council of Trent and First Vatican Council," all that was involved was presenting that teaching in such a way as to respond to the needs of the time and to that end displaying "a Magisterium which is predominantly pastoral in character." From the other point of view, the Church of today preferred "to make use of the medicine of mercy rather than that of severity," and therefore considered that, rather than condemn, she would better respond to "the needs of the present day by demonstrating the validity of her teaching."[1]

The acoustics were excellent, and the pope spoke perfectly. Even so, until he saw the text itself, at the end of the day, Cardinal Siri did not know whether he had been dreaming. On the other hand, Congar did not grasp the implications of what he had heard and left before the end

---

[1] *Gaudet Mater Ecclesia*, no. 7.

of the ceremony, disgusted by its "Constantinian" aspect. The pope's softly phrased cancellation of the spirit and the letter of the projects prepared by the staff of Pius XII, who still ran the Curia, had not been enough to bring things home to him, so difficult was it to imagine such a radical turnaround in the nature of the supreme Magisterium before its effects were clearly visible. A new era was starting, in which the way that the Church had thought of herself ever since the Gregorian reform would now be obsolete.

The battle over procedure was launched, and won two days later by the French and the Germans, who wanted to stop the Curia from locking down the activity of the assembly. Specifically, this required the French and the Germans to prevent the prelates and experts nominated by the Curia from forming a majority on the commissions, and especially on the Commission on Doctrine. Ottaviani's intention was in general terms to keep in place those who had participated in the committees of the preparatory stage. The Fathers of the Council, although they had complete freedom to vote, nevertheless found themselves presented with the list of the members of the preparatory commissions, who were in some sense official candidates, recommended by their competence and by their papal nomination.

The story has been repeated dozens of times, on each occasion with increased detail, as those involved have let drop revelations on this "legal putsch." Monsignor Garrone, whose idea it was, set "to work" Cardinal Eugène Tisserant who, as the first of the presiding prelates was to oversee the opening session. Monsignor Garrone also succeeded in convincing Cardinal Liénart, Bishop of Lille, who was also on the presiding council, to ask for the elections to be adjourned. That would allow the best organized of the various lobbying parties, namely the European episcopal conferences, to put forward lists of candidates who would be the "opposition" candidates.

Cardinal Liénart gave way, and after asking to speak at the start of the first General Congregation, read out a short intervention (prepared by the liturgist Aimé-Georges Martimort and passed on to the Cardinal by Monsignor Garrone). The proposition, immediately supported by Cardinal Joseph Frings, of Cologne, as expected, was accepted after a brief consultation by Cardinal Tisserant and by Monsignor Pericle Felici, the secretary of the assembly. The right had been outwitted by sleight of hand, and was dumbfounded when it realized how popular this "anti-Roman" coup was.

Ottaviani did not react until October 16, the day appointed for the vote, when he tried to regain the initiative, but without having prepared the ground beforehand: he proposed, supposedly to speed things up, a complex modification of the rules governing the election, which would in practice have given the advantage to the Italians, thanks to their solid block of 480 bishops, presided over, and for the moment kept sufficiently under control, by Cardinal Siri of Genoa. Oblivious to the danger, Cardinal Ruffini opposed the proposal, for all the world as if it were a minor academic tussle between specialists over a point of procedure.

By contrast, the liberal wing had not wasted a minute. Lists had circulated, and there had been many negotiations, notably between the European and African episcopal conferences. If the results of the elections did not immediately appear to be a triumph—and that was all the more difficult to measure since the Fathers were not signed up as members of parties as they would be in a parliamentary assembly—they nevertheless marked the end of the supremacy of the Curia. John XXIII, whose task it was according to the procedures to finalize the membership of the commissions, and who could have restored the position of the Holy Office in the Commission on Doctrine, made a "balanced" series of appointments, that is to say, appointments which did not in any way modify the new position. It quickly became clear that on October 13, 1962 the balance of power had shifted substantially and definitively.

So the battle over the examination of the texts was now launched. Twenty schemata were ready to be submitted to the Council for discussion. Four were due to be presented first: *De Fontibus Revelationis*, on the sources of Revelation; *De Ecclesiae Unitate*, on the unity of the Church, prepared by the Commission of the Oriental Churches (and therefore distinct from the text on ecumenism prepared by the Secretariat for Christian Unity); *De Instrumentis Diffusionis seu Communicationis Socialis*, on communications media; and last the notorious *De Ecclesia.*

De Fontibus and *De Ecclesia*, along with the schemata *De Castitate, Virginitate, Matrimonio, Familia*, on chastity, virginity, marriage, and the family; *De Ordine Morali*, on the Christian moral order; *De Deposito Fidei Pure Custodiendo*, on defending the deposit of faith; and *De Beata Maria Virgine Matre Dei et Matre Hominum*, on the Blessed Virgin Mary; formed part of the projected dogmatic constitutions prepared by the Theological Commission and which, in the thinking of their authors, were to constitute the backbone of Vatican II. However, counter-proposals were already being circulated. During the previous summer, Edward Schillebeeckx, a Dominican of Flemish origin and professor at the Catholic University of Nijmegen, had put together a very critical paper. Adopted by seventeen Dutch bishops, the analysis had been widely circulated among the bishops arriving in Rome. Since it had been translated into French and English, many bishops read it even before they had become acquainted with the official schemata which were distributed in Latin.

Schillebeeckx's paper contained one objective to which the "progressive" party was greatly attached: this was that discussion should start, not with the doctrinal schemata, but with the schema on the liturgy, *De Sacra Liturgia*, which by reason of its practical subject-matter and the orientation of its authors, had nothing "scholastic" about it. Cardinals Joseph Frings, Achille Liénart, and Bernard Alfrink (of Utrecht), who were all members of the Council's presiding body, ensured that this schema was the first to be examined. Debate lasted almost a month and ended, not with a vote on a text, but with the almost unanimous adoption of relatively vague general principles. To tell the truth, the project presented did not wholly satisfy anyone, but in the eyes of the right its only fault was its generally reformist tenor, which could, they thought, be channeled in the correct direction.

From this point on it was unthinkable that it would be possible to deliver a council following in the lines of *Humani Generis*. But it was still not an absolute given that the council would throw the discussion open. So there was still a possibility of a council that would achieve nothing, the last hope of "the Curia," the expression that was used from now on to describe the party that found itself in the minority. This was in fact the great fear of the liberals, as is witnessed by all the confidential briefings that they gave at the time.

The real effect of the debate on the liturgy was that there were no limits to the discussion and so the participants realized that everything was now up for debate, and that even the boldest proposals, such as rewriting the Canon of the Mass, could be put forward. People debated about the usage of Latin and of the vernacular, about concelebrations—occasionally, frequently, or not at all—about the eucharistic fast, about the Sunday obligation, about Communion under the species of wine, about the simplification of the liturgy, and about the reduction in length of the Divine Office. There were particularly bitter debates over the general theme of whether to allow necessary adaptation or maintain strict continuity. On October 30 occurred the episode of the humiliation of the cardinal scapegoat. Ottaviani was warning that the Christian people would be gravely disturbed if the rite of the Mass was treated "as a piece of cloth that is refashioned to suit the taste of each succeeding generation." Since he had exceeded the time allowed for his speech, Cardinal Alfrink cut off his microphone, and Ottaviani, reduced to silence, had to resume his place amidst the cruel applause of the majority. For good measure, Patriarch Maximos IV, one of the Curia's most open adversaries, was allowed to speak for fifty minutes on November 27 without interruption.

It was in this atmosphere of insurrection that grew ever more sure of itself that the schema *De Fontibus Revelationis*, on the sources of Revelation, arrived before the assembly. It was rather awkwardly exposed to criticism as the result of some defensive drafting that suggested that in scriptural matters it had concerns about the openings in Pius XII's encyclical *Divino Afflante*. These were points that, to be honest, could easily have been corrected: the proof of this is, that whatever was said on the subject, the constitution *Dei Verbum* of November 18, 1965, which replaced the rejected schema, was based on a theology substantially the same as that of the initial text. In the short term, the schema underwent so intense a barrage of fire that discussion of the text was replaced by discussion of whether it should be purely and simply sent back for rewriting. A counter-schema, prepared by the Jesuit Karl Rahner, a theological advisor to the German episcopal conference, with the assistance of the theologians Joseph Ratzinger, Aloys Grillmeier, and Otto Semmelroth, was in circulation and was the subject of debate among the French, Dutch, Belgian, Swiss, and Austrian bishops. Ottaviani's poignant response was, "What right have they?" On the opposite side of the divide, Monsignor De Smedt, of Brussels, was the first to use against the curial text the argument against which there was no appeal and which would be used thereafter until it was positively threadbare, "The schema is notably lacking in ecumenical spirit!" Later on, Congar, observing the progress that had been made, humorously commented that it was sufficient to invoke the argument "It's ecumenical!" or "It isn't ecumenical!" to get a proposal adopted or rejected.

Don Giuseppe Dossetti, one of the leading post-war Christian Democrat politicians, who later took Holy Orders, and who was an advisor to Cardinal Giacomo Lercaro of Bologna, explained that in his experience the victories were won on the battlefield of procedure. The stakes in this battle forced the right into a reassessment. All its leading voices, Ottaviani, Antonio Bacci, Michael Browne, who was the General of the Dominicans, Siri, and Fernando Quiroga y Palacios, of Saint James of Compostella, spoke up for the prepared text. Miraculously, they even showed a certain tactical ability in the parliamentary context in which they found themselves trapped. Since the rule required that a procedural motion should receive two thirds of the votes to be accepted, Cardinal Ruffini ensured that the question related not to the continuance of the discussion ("Does the Council decide to undertake the discussion of the schema?") but to the rejection of the text ("Does the Council decide to send the schema back?"). Then, in the disorder that preceded the vote, he ingeniously persuaded his fellows that a rejection of the text meant quite simply a refusal to treat the theme of Revelation in the Council.

On November 20, 1962, the fate of the Council hung in the balance. The motion for a rejection obtained only a simple majority, and not the necessary two-thirds majority. The minority had the power to bring movement to a halt. This was its only success, and one that was very short-lived, since on the following day, without doubt at the instigation of Cardinal Paul-Émile Léger, Archbishop of Montreal, and coached by Cardinal Montini and Cardinal Léon-Joseph Suenens, Archbishop of Malines-Brussels, the pope announced that the discussion was adjourned and that a new text would be prepared by a joint commission composed of members of the Doctrinal

Commission and—to the consternation of some—of members of the Secretariat for Christian Unity, presided over by Cardinal Bea. One could ask what made such a commission competent to treat of Revelation, other than that it embodied the new way of thinking.

The rejection of the other curial texts followed logically. *De Unitate Ecclesiae*, presented by the Commission for the Oriental Churches, was returned to be amalgamated with the schema prepared by the Theological Commission and above all with that prepared by the Secretariat for Christian Unity, which became a sort of alternative Holy Office. There were only a few days left before the end of the session in which to examine *De Ecclesia*. There was an outcry: the text was "triumphalist," it was not "open-minded," it was "unecumenical" and "legalist." With an authority that was very revealing of the majority's new realization of its own power, Cardinal Suenens developed a plan, examined beforehand by the pope, for a rethinking of the whole work of the Council: it would be necessary to consider the Church *ad intra* and *ad extra*, focusing on missionary activity, on her relationship to other Christian communities, and on her concern for the problems of contemporary man: hunger, war, the "population explosion," etc.

When the bishops took their leave of each other, they had therefore not elaborated a single text. They had only voted on the introduction and the first chapter of the Constitution on the Sacred Liturgy, with its paragraph 40: "It is urgent to adapt the liturgy more profoundly." A "new wind" was passing over the Church. The victorious party seemed enlarged by many hesitant new adherents. In reality these were deserters from the traditionalist party. The conservatism—especially the liturgical conservatism—of the American bishops started to weaken, and the Spanish, Mexican, and Argentinian group of bishops appeared much less monolithic than had been thought. The great mass of bishops returned to their dioceses as supporters of change and almost in a state of euphoria over the battle into which they had been conscripted. A Guinean bishop, who had left as a conservative and returned as a progressivist, exclaimed proudly to his priests "We fought against Ottaviani!" It was only then that the theologians of the "movement," Congar, Küng, the all-powerful Rahner, who combined his doubtless sincere passion for the Church with another of an entirely different order, Gustave Martelet, Henri Rondet, and Chenu, all allowed themselves to be overcome with optimism. "I must admit it," wrote Father Robert Rouquette, chronicler of the Council for *La Croix*, "I arrived in Rome, at the start of October, pessimistic about what we could expect from the Council. I am leaving it, after it has been in session for two months, completely overwhelmed by having taken part in a great historic event, a decisive turning-point in the history of the Church."

Conversely, the members of the minority, who had lost the war as well as the battle, were knocked flat. "We have opened the door to Luther, to rationalism, and to modernism," cried Ruffini, after Ottaviani's last scheme had failed. In essence, Ottaviani had made the most important point when he introduced *De Fontibus Revelationis*: what was being discussed was a doctrinal text which, if the Church intended to preserve the deposit of faith, required her to manifest her vigilance. She needed to accompany the text with a condemnation of the errors which put this deposit in danger. Now it was precisely that action that had been jettisoned: from now on it was understood that Vatican II would not be one of those councils aimed at "preservation without impairment," with their doctrinal formulations and their accompanying denunciations of heterodox propositions.

Just to confirm this message, John XXIII, in his reply of December 23 to the seasonal greeting of the Sacred College, took up again in a still clearer fashion the central theme of his opening address. He was replying implicitly to Cardinal Siri, who had tried to give a reassuring interpretation of the results of the first session: "The purpose of the Council is not to discuss this or that article of the Church's fundamental doctrine." The pope added that today this doctrine had to be promulgated "following the methods of research and the literary formulation of modern thought," and to be expressed "in accordance with the needs of a magisterium whose character is above all pastoral."[2] Vatican II would not be *a council*: it was *the Council*.

---

[2] *La Documentation catholique*, vol. 60, no. 1392, 20 January 1963, col. 101.

CHAPTER 8

A New State of Affairs

BETWEEN THE REVERSAL that occurred at the first session and the creation of the principal texts that established "the spirit of Vatican II" at the third and fourth sessions, there was an intermediate phase, the second session, which was distinguished by two events: the election of a new pope who would from now on actually take control of the new state of affairs rather than just give it a genial blessing, and the working out of the first stages of a doctrine in shades of grey, the doctrine of collegiality, that would be superimposed on a doctrine in bold colors.

The election of Paul VI on June 21, 1963, seemed so natural that some sycophantic voices spoke of a vote "by inspiration" (a method of election which was then possible and in which the cardinals choose the successful candidate by acclamation, without even proceeding to a vote). This was quite wrong since there is no doubt that the decision was only reached with difficulty. A survey of the situation at the conclave which met after the death of John XXIII will allow us to observe the complex balance of forces. The *papabile* of the right, Cardinal Ildebrando Antoniutti, supported by Cardinals Ruffini, Ottaviani, and above all Siri, could not hope to be elected, but he could have blocked the election of Montini. In a conclave, since a two-thirds majority is required (at the time, two-thirds plus one), if one third of the electors are firmly resolved to bar a candidate, they are enough to put an end to even the most confident predictions. This was the tactic put into operation by Cardinal Siri. It seems that he was on the point of succeeding, but he failed to persuade his supporters to follow it through right to the end. If

Cardinal Montini had been sidelined, negotiations would have been necessary, and the right could have lent their support to a candidate capable of frustrating the Council. The atmosphere of the conclave was extremely tense and, according to the account of Cardinal Siri, even dramatic, with the party that he inspired willing to stake everything on blocking the upset that was in process.

The two groupings therefore faced each other, the conciliar and the anti-conciliar. We must repeat clearly that the terms left and right are only used for the sake of convenience, and describe in schematic terms a reality that was far more complex, with matters already being far from simple at the heart of the "conciliars." If we are to understand fully what happened at Vatican II, its consequences, and the reasons for its survival, we must always keep in mind, that whatever the importance of the reversal that had been achieved in the previous autumn, that reversal was—because it could not be otherwise—a moderate revolution. From 1963 and right up to our own day, two parties struggle for power in the camp of the winners, a moderate conciliar tendency, represented at the conclave by Cardinal Montini, and a tendency that is mistakenly referred to as "progressive," since in fact doctrinal modernism is much more important within it than the Marxist sympathies which are the mark of progressivism properly so called. This second party, regarded as of the "left," but in reality composed of advanced liberals, was at the time represented by Cardinal Lercaro (it would later be represented by Cardinal Carlo Maria Martini and then by Pope Francis). It could only, and can only, retain control by moderating its most advanced claims in order to avoid a complete collapse of its authority. But from the time of the Council and in the succeeding period it has exerted constant pressure, like yeast in the conciliar dough, either by directly and powerfully supporting the advance of reforms, or on the contrary by using, in a rather enigmatic way, the theological "excesses" and the liturgical "abuses" of its extreme members as a foil. The result is that for the new ecclesiastical settlement to last, it has absolutely to be maintained from the center, the center-right, or the center-left, requiring subtle calculations: Montini the moderate, once elected, left the direction of a neutered Holy Office to the integrist Ottaviani, and entrusted the oversight of the liturgical reform to the progressivist Lercaro.

Under canon law, the Council had been terminated by the death of the pope, and it was theoretically possible for a new pope not to reconvene it. But Paul VI hastened to announce, on the day after his election, that it would continue. From now on, Vatican II had a leader. An intellectual of good standing, a convinced disciple of Jacques Maritain, he had under Pius XII been an advisor to the leaders of the Italian Christian Democratic party and the organizers of the Christian trade unions. After 1950 he had, with great circumspection, made clear his disagreement with *Humani Generis*. He was criticized for his hesitancy: it is possible that the semi-disgrace represented by his nomination to the see of Milan was due not only to his theological opinions, but also to the difficulty that he experienced in making important decisions.

Now this characteristic hesitancy, which made decisions painful for Paul VI, was perhaps his most valuable trait. His opponents on the right generally regard him as more of an innovator than he actually was. Certainly his indecisive prudence was the best trump card that he could have had in ensuring the viability of the Council. His great concern was to obtain votes that were nearly unanimous, and to achieve this he would mollify as much as he could the concerns of the minority. As soon as he had been elected, he arranged for the introduction of amendments which numerous voices among the majority instantly termed "regrettable." He thus smoothed down some of the rougher points of the schema on ecumenism, and he removed the questions of priestly celibacy and birth control from the conciliar agenda. This last subject had, during the week of November 21 to 28, given rise to maneuvers aimed at revisiting the teaching contained in Pius XII's encyclical *Casti Connubii* of December 31, 1930, instigated by Philippe Delhaye, Charles De Koninck, and Pierre De Locht. Discussion of the matter was therefore reserved to the pope, and a note was added to the constitution *Gaudium et Spes*, discussing conjugal love and respect for human life. The note, which related to the third paragraph of § 51, "For children of the Church, taking their stand on these principles, it is not lawful to regulate procreation by embarking in ways which the Church's teaching authority, in expounding the divine law, condemns," added the qualification, "Certain questions which need other and more careful investigation have been submitted by command of the pope to a Commission for the study of population, family, and birth questions, so that the Supreme Pontiff may give judgment when the commission has finished its work. In view of this the Council does not intend immediately to propose concrete solutions."[1] As is well known, Paul VI gave his response with the encyclical *Humanae Vitae* of July 25, 1968. Additionally, at the end of the third session, he decided on his own authority to decree that the title "Mother of the Church" should be awarded to the Holy Virgin, even though this title had been removed from the chapter of the Constitution on the Church dedicated to the Virgin Mary.[2] Paul arranged for this constitution to be completed with a *nota explicativa praevia*, a preliminary explanatory note, which made clear the relationship between the powers of the pope and those of the College of Bishops.[3]

---

[1] Paul VI, Pastoral Constitution *Gaudium et Spes*, December 7, 1965, no. 51, n. 118.

[2] Second Vatican Council, Constitution *Lumen Gentium*, November 21, 1964, nos. 53, 61; Paul VI, Address at the Closing of the Third Session, November 21, 1964, *Acta Apostolicae Sedis* LVI (1964), 1016.

[3] *Lumen Gentium*, Appendix.

Paul VI remodeled the governing structure of the Council by doubling in size the presiding group of four moderators, who took turns in leading the debates (Cardinals Pietro Agagianian; Julius Döpfner, Archbishop of Munich; Lercaro; and Suenens). He created a plan for the Council's work and modified its procedures so as to avoid any possibility of a procedural impasse. In particular, he changed the rules which required a two-thirds majority for a rejection or the complete adjournment of a schema. In this way, given that the "movement" could from now on always be relied on to have a majority, it became impossible—however the questions put to the assembly were phrased—for the minority to succeed in paralyzing the debates. We should add that his election loosened the authority which Cardinal Siri had enjoyed at the center of the Italian episcopate, something which caused the minority to lose an important source of votes. In his opening address to the second session of the Council the pope turned his back on the attitude established by *Humani Generis*, which was the cross that he had borne while under the shadow of Pius XII. He made the objectives of the assembly clear: the renewal of the Church, the promotion of Christian unity, and dialogue with the modern world. He confirmed that the framework for the work of the Council was its "pastoral" character, something which would allow the Council, while avoiding the "condemnation of errors," to "build a bridge to the contemporary world."[4]

The texts which the Council produced from now on were quite varied. Some of them, in whole or in part, are relatively similar to the general expositions of the First Vatican Council, with the one difference that those texts concluded with canons summarizing the doctrine that had been put forward and anathemas condemning the

[4] *Concilio propositum est, ut humanam consortionem nostrae aetatis, quodam quasi ponte instituto, attingat* (Paul VI, Address at the beginning of the Second Session, September 29, 1963).

contrasting errors. In fact, the general style employed by Vatican II remains quite close to that of the encyclicals of Pius XII, even though the editors of Vatican II thought that they were being very innovative in their mode of expression. If we compare, for example, one of the key passages of the constitution *Dei Verbum*, discussing the inspiration of Holy Scripture, its interpretation, and the literary genres represented, it feels as if we are reading the corresponding passage of the encyclical *Divino Afflante*. We find the same quotations from Saint Augustine on the way in which God talks to men and from Saint John Chrysostom on the divine "condescension" used and made the subject of commentary in an identical fashion. What is generally characteristic of the conciliar editors at their best is their way of introducing and using the scriptural and patristic quotations in the form of a reasonably successful paraphrase. It is true that the contemporary reader would be happier with formulations that are less verbose and better minted. If we add the numerous passages where the pen made many tentative dips into the inkwell in order to say what was wanted without saying what was not wanted, or even to say several things at one and the same time, and the incorporation with scissors and paste of the most varied amendments, we are forced to admit that there are numerous repetitions and the clarity of the "pastoral" message sometimes suffers.

This was the general framework within which numerous minor changes would be introduced, all of which, to different degrees, are the product of an attitude that we need to grasp if we are to understand how the Church's traditional doctrinal function was neutralized. We encounter an attitude of a voluntary refusal in the Church's supreme teaching function, a sort of abdication aimed at creating an "openness" toward the world. Two examples of this abdication, which we can mark as of minor importance, can be quoted if we anticipate the Council's final completion, since both of them were only finally decided on in the fourth session. Although they are of minor importance in comparison with the great "intuitions," they are characteristic of the change that was taking place.

The first example is well known and is almost a caricature of the type. It is the treatment of communism in the constitution *Gaudium et Spes*. This constitution is certainly the worst conciliar text from the stylistic point of view, and it foreshadows the wooden language of the post-conciliar era with its vague and over-rhetorical analyses that blend the sociological and the spiritual. This text, an indelible stain on the memory of Vatican II, and dealing with "the Church in today's world," only includes a single reference, allusive, and as euphemistic as possible, without even daring to use its name, to that criminal ideology which was enslaving half the planet and oppressing religion in an overt persecution:

> In her loyal devotion to God and men, the Church has already repudiated and cannot cease repudiating, sorrowfully but as firmly as possible, those poisonous doctrines and actions which contradict reason and the common experience of humanity, and dethrone man from his native excellence.

Shocked by their own boldness, the conciliar Fathers nevertheless at once watered down what they had just said:

> Still, she strives to detect in the atheistic mind the hidden causes for the denial of God; conscious of how weighty are the questions which atheism raises, and motivated by love for all men, she believes these questions ought to be examined seriously and more profoundly.[5]

In all decency and respect for the martyrs, would it not have been better to say nothing at all?

---

[5] *Gaudium et Spes*, no. 21.

In the second example, the Council had its eyes fixed, no longer on the communist world, but on the Protestants. The minority, with the support in this instance of numerous bishops animated by Marian piety, was exceptionally keen that the Council should make a definition relative to the Virgin Mary. In the time of Pius XII, there had often been mention of defining her co-redemption, or of her universal mediation of all graces. When the time came for the Council, people spoke with greater willingness, in debates between Mariologists that are completely forgotten today, about defining "the spiritual motherhood of Mary." This focus of papal infallibility on the Holy Virgin was capable of prompting numerous reservations, because it suggested that the usage of the supreme Magisterium consisted of little more than these very occasional definitions, the Immaculate Conception, the Assumption, both in the past, and in the future the Spiritual Maternity. It brought out above all the extreme unease of the majority, who were afraid of irritating the Protestants and considered that it was quite the wrong time to get involved on this particular battlefield. That was most notably the advice of the German experts, Aloys Grillmeier, Joseph Ratzinger, and Karl Rahner, who were afraid that a definition, and a Mariological one at that, would be slipped in surreptitiously, and insisted that the *De Beata Virgine Maria* should be incorporated into the Constitution on the Church (it had been separated in the course of the preparatory studies, in March 1962). The title "Mediatrix" was therefore weakened by the addition of three other titles as equivalents (Advocate, Auxiliatrix, and Adjutrix), surrounded by precautionary references to the unique mediation of Christ, and finally relativized by a preliminary declaration that the Council had no intention of coming to any definitive decision whatsoever.[6] Even that was too much for the Protestants: speaking on their behalf, the very moderate

[6] *Lumen Gentium*, no. 62.

Oscar Cullmann regretted that the chapter on Mary, now endowed with the anti-ecumenical title of "Mediatrix," was placed at the end of the Constitution on the Church, as if that were its culminating point.

Irritating as these "silences" of the Council generally are, and woefully scandalous as is the absence of prophetic courage faced with the communist tyranny, it can nevertheless be argued that the assembly was the sole judge of whether it was the moment to repeat the condemnation of an ideology, or to advance toward a Marian definition for which there was no pressing urgency. The instances nevertheless show in a specific way that there was a close link between the attitude of resignation from the point of view of teaching and the desire for an "openness towards contemporary man." This abstention was going to become much heavier with consequences in the areas in which Vatican II prepared itself to make new doctrinal points. That is why the discussion on, and the working out of, the text on episcopal collegiality come much closer than the two examples just mentioned to the major problem raised by Vatican II. In itself, the affirmation that all the bishops of the world, united with the pope and under his authority, form a college which exercises the pastoral responsibility of the Church, contains nothing shocking. Quite the contrary, it allowed a rebalancing of a theology and, in consequence, of a conception of the life of the Church, which had developed a very real tendency to overemphasize one of the poles of its divine constitution, the pope, to the detriment of the other, the bishops.

In general terms, the opposition's amendments, whenever they proposed fundamental modifications, were defeated. The ambiguity was therefore located within the conciliar text: "The order of Bishops is the successor to the college of the apostles.... "[7] It was hardly reduced by the replacement of one term (the "order" of Bishops and not the "College," showing that the succession

---

[7] Ibid., no. 22.

could be interpreted in a loose way: replacement of one authority by another). The preliminary explanatory note, which Paul VI had published in the last week of the third session in order to reassure the bishops of the minority party, reaffirmed the doctrine of papal supremacy but took care not to dispel the fuzziness on the subject of the apostolic succession. This productive indecision from then on became part of irreversible established doctrine. To tell the truth, it had acquired a psychological significance for its supporters and opponents that was much greater than any decisive doctrinal importance. In any case, everything took place as if doctrinal authority was already immobilized, with the guardian of dogmatic rigor, the pope, locking away his own power of decision.

The power of the Holy Office, the unique instrument of the Sovereign Pontiff's function of deciding on matters of the faith, was shattered for good by the blows of its adversaries. On November 5, Cardinal Browne, vice-president of the Doctrinal Commission and spokesman for Cardinal Ottaviani, criticized the proposals of the moderators which the Fathers had adopted. On November 8, Cardinal Frings, who like his adversary Cardinal Ottaviani was practically blind, rose formally to oppose this claim: the Doctrinal Commission, he said, was merely an instrument of the Council. He went on, interrupted several times by the applause of the majority, to accuse the Holy Office of judging and condemning its opponents without a hearing, and of using "methods that did not correspond to modern conditions." Cardinal Ottaviani replied formally, pointing out to him that to attack the Holy Office, of which he was merely the Pro-Prefect, was to attack the pope himself. A fruitless defense, since it was clear that the pope supported the party represented by Cardinal Frings.

This debate on episcopal collegiality of October and November 1963, arising out of the examination of the draft of the constitution *Lumen Gentium* and of the decree

Christus Dominus on the responsibilities of bishops, a debate which would flare up again vehemently in the third session, was an important stage on the way events unfolded: it demonstrated how, in a manner of speaking, Rome had abandoned her central position.

What is more, while this displacement was taking place, another simultaneous movement, which took note of the first, was occurring in the conciliar minority: the hard core opposition to the course of Vatican II was distancing itself from the Roman center. Up until this moment, the minority had been identified with the Curia. But when it became clear that it was fighting against the pope's preferences, this curial party lost its edge, as if its legitimacy were progressively vanishing before its very eyes. Of course, it continued to listen to the weighty voices of Cardinals Ottaviani, Browne, Ruffini, and even more the very emotive voice of Cardinal Siri, who organized quite an effective counter-effort focused on the bishops who spoke Italian, Spanish, or Portuguese. Nevertheless, the defense of the traditional positions would from now on be essentially undertaken by peripheral and less well-known bishops, who now moved forward to the front line. Monsignor Geraldo de Proença Sigaud, Archbishop of Dimantina, in Brazil, and Monsignor Luigi-Maria Carli, Bishop of Segni, in Italy, came to the notice of the assembly when they made their respective interventions on the subject of the ambiguity of the references to collegiality. Monsignor Marcel Lefebvre, previously Archbishop of Dakar (then, for some months in 1962, Archbishop-bishop of Tulle), who had become the Superior of the Fathers of the Holy Spirit, had already with the Brazilian archbishop formed a small coordinating committee. Certainly, they retained a connection with the Vatican administration, in the person of Monsignor Dino Staffa, who was Secretary of the Congregation of Seminaries and Cardinal Pizzardo's closest collaborator. With the addition of some others, such as Monsignor

Antonio de Castro Mayer, Bishop of Campos, in Brazil, they established a *Coetus Internationalis Patrum* (which later became the *Coetus Episcopalis Patrum*), which organized weekly conferences, first in the house of the Augustinian Fathers, opposite the Holy Office, then at the Hotel Columbus, on the *via della Conciliazone*, and finally they published a newsletter.

Despite its resources being ridiculously weak in comparison with those enjoyed by the European episcopal conferences who were orchestrating the debates, the *Coetus* observed, little by little, that it was becoming the focus of the animosity which the majority felt toward the now fatally wounded Curia. A well-known vicious circle worked against them: the clumsy actions of a group banished to the sidelines gave rise to mistrust; the mistrust forced the group into actions that failed to measure up to events themselves. For example, in arranging for seminarians to hand out leaflets to the Council Fathers as they arrived for a session, the *Coetus* confirmed conciliar Rome's impression of amateur protests that would stick to integrist groups in the period following the Council, a period dominated by Paul VI.

It was not until the third session that some cardinals, initially Rufino Santos, of Manila, and then Ruffini, Siri, Larraona, and Brown, dared to reveal themselves as their allies, but in something of a supporting position. The situation, of course, was entirely new, and foreshadowed that which would exist after the Council: the claim that doctrine was permanently valid could no longer coexist with the fiction that doctrine originated with the pope. Its defenders were forced to reorient themselves, not without hesitations and some agony, on the lines of the French integrist Catholicism that had opposed Rome's political instructions: a papism that was opposed to the pope. In a certain way, it would be integrist Catholicism that from now on assumed the leadership of the opposition to the conciliar movement.

CHAPTER 9

The Spirit of the Council

THREE TEXTS, WHICH to begin with were just a single text, are the basis of what is commonly called "the Spirit of the Council": the decree *Unitatis Redintegratio*, on ecumenism; the declaration *Nostra Aetate*, on the relationship between the Church and non-Christian religions; and the declaration *Dignitatis Humanae*, promulgated on the last day of the Council, which, without being very dense or particularly coherent, would be, in comparison with the others, the Second Vatican Council's principal text. Of course, we cannot deny the importance of Schema XIII, on "the Church in the Modern World," which became the pastoral constitution *Gaudium et Spes*. But Schema XIII was as it were the decorative surrounding to the Church's opening to the world. *Gaudium et Spes* is all the same a complex text, disjointed, prolix, and—we must admit it—fairly insignificant. From the doctrinal point of view, it was the productions of the Secretariat for Christian Unity that occupied the foreground.

Cardinal Bea's secretariat presented its draft of the single text at the second session, in the autumn of 1963, when it still included a chapter on non-Christian religions, specifically on Judaism, and another on religious freedom. It was during the break that followed the second session that these two topics were detached so that they could be developed into two other independent texts.

Ecumenism was therefore the central kernel. The body of the decree on ecumenism, promulgated at the end of the third session, had been essentially approved, without great difficulty, at the second session. It is a quite astonishing document: this text of twenty four paragraphs does not contain the slightest doctrinal definition, not even an indirect one, of ecumenism. The decree only contains, as we have already seen, this articulation of ecumenical practice: "By 'ecumenical movement' we understand the activities and initiatives called into being and organized with a view to the unity of Christians."

As we have seen, beginning in the preparatory period, it was a deliberate decision that the sub-commission charged with working up a doctrinal formulation should conclude that it would be more suitable to prepare a practical text rather than a doctrinal one. "In Rome," said Canon Gustave Thils, "people are readier to accept concrete proposals and practical solutions than they are to accept a theological disquisition." And Monsignor De Smedt went one step further: "Is ecumenical theology sufficiently mature for us to be able to work up a doctrinal decree?" It was necessary therefore to act, while postponing the elaboration of a theory of action until a later period: today, matters are practically in their original state. The decree thus avoided giving an answer to the fundamental question: once all the difficulties and reciprocal misunderstandings have been smoothed out by ecumenical discussions, will Christian unity be obtained by the return of non-Catholic Christians to the Catholic Church? In other words, the decree took care not to make the objective explicit: What sort of unity was being sought? This was an essential feature, as we have seen, of the Secretariat's method of proceeding: in order for there to be a Catholic ecumenism which was neither a development of the traditional unionism, nor an openly heterodox course of action (the march toward a sort of federal Church which would incorporate the reunited Christian denominations), it was necessary to work out a "pastoral" third way, while treating the traditional doctrine with a certain legerdemain. But the text goes beyond ambiguity when it forges the novel idea of "imperfect communion" with the Catholic Church, from which separated Christians benefit, and when it affirms that the separated Churches and communities, insofar as they are separated, and not because of the elements of sanctification which in fact are present within them, can be "means of salvation," whose effectiveness derives from the Catholic Church.[1] The separated Christians—it is not clear that they would be happy with this euphemism—would be partial Catholics, and their Churches and communities would be as it were incomplete offshoots of Catholicism.

The minority, being entirely occupied by the question of collegiality, a theme which was all the more familiar to it because it concerned the powers of the Roman Pontiff, hardly focused its attention during the Council itself on the theme of ecumenism. Concerned nevertheless about the "mistaken interpretations" that might arise, the minority pressured Paul VI who, *in extremis*, asked for the introduction of a series of amendments which he thought would restore peace, with a view to obtaining the necessary overwhelming vote of favor needed for a text of this importance. And in the event, the decree *Unitatis Redintegratio* was passed almost unanimously, on November 21, 1964, with 2,137 votes for and 11 votes against.

Approval of the declaration *Nostra Aetate* on relations with non-Christian religions was definitely more difficult. The principal cause of this was the debates focused on Judaism: could the Jewish people, as a people, be held responsible for the death of Christ that had been instigated by its chiefs? It is well-known that the Council avoided the question by saying, "Even though the Jewish authorities, with their supporters, pushed for the death of Christ, the actions carried out during his passion cannot be imputed, either indiscriminately to all the Jews then alive, or to the Jews of our own day."[2] In fact, given the

---

1 *Unitatis Redintegratio*, no. 3.

2 Second Vatican Council, Declaration *Nostra Aetate*, October 28,

concern to avoid causing unnecessary offence to Muslim countries, considerations affecting the Jews occupied a lesser proportion than originally anticipated of the attention devoted to questions relating to the entirety of the non-Christian religions. The opening to the world required some skillful balancing of emphases.

The consequences of what would soon be called the theology of religions, like those of the theology of ecumenism, later ran into what might be called the "air pockets" of the Council. In this case, the vacuum relates very precisely to this: the declaration on the non-Christian religions does not make clear who the partners in dialogue are. If we take the words of the conciliar document at face value, we might conclude that interreligious dialogue sets up a relationship with men of good will belonging in point of fact to the non-Christian religions themselves rather than with the non-Christian religions themselves or with their authorized representatives:

> The Church, therefore, exhorts her sons, that through dialogue and collaboration with the followers of other religions, carried out with prudence and love and in witness to the Christian faith and life, they recognize, preserve and promote the good things, spiritual and moral, as well as the socio-cultural values found among these men.[3]

But the text does not stop there. It goes on to say, and above all:

> The Catholic Church rejects nothing that is true and holy in these religions. She regards with sincere reverence those ways of conduct and of life, those precepts and teachings which, though differing in many aspects from the ones she holds

1965, no. 4.

[3] Ibid., no. 2.

> and sets forth, nonetheless often reflect a ray of that Truth which enlightens all men.

Sincera cum observantia [with sincere reverence] *considerat... illa præcepta et doctrina*, says the Latin text. The usual French translations render *observantia*, which is more than a simple *respectus* (which would already cause difficulties) by *respect sincère*, which is too weak. It would be better to translate what the Council has said, in this context, by *respect religieux* [sacred respect] (see 2 Mac 6:11, in the Vulgate version, where some Jews allowed themselves to be burnt alive in caves because of the sacred respect—*ob religionem et observantiam*—with which they regarded the Sabbath).

In any hypothesis, whether we translate the phrase as "sacred respect" or just as "respect," it is here that we find the problem that *Nostra Aetate* places in the path of a peaceful Catholic reception: there is a logical and theological leap from the particular to the general. Nobody denies that the non-Christian religions can contain elements of the truth. Everyone agrees that these elements, taken on their own, and what is more, carefully distinguished in the preaching of missionaries, can constitute stepping-stones toward Revelation. But are these rays of truth not hidden in the midst of errors of every sort, which do not deserve any "respect"? Is not the worst of these errors exactly the fact that the systems that imprison these fragments of truth falsely claim to be "religions," that is, means of salvation? It is difficult to understand how an ecumenical Council can teach that these false means of salvation should be treated with "sincere respect."

The rogue wave that this generated was such that *La Civiltà Cattolica*, the journal of the Roman Jesuits that is regarded as the mouthpiece of the Secretariat of State, was able to say calmly, "Non-Christian religious traditions are 'extraordinary means' of salvation by reason of the elements found in them which can be the fruit of the presence in them of the Holy Spirit."[4] Further still, on the subject of books held sacred by other religions, such as the Qur'an, "We can maintain that, being written by men who were profoundly religious, and not without some guidance from the Holy Spirit, they consequently contain, to a certain extent, a 'divine revelation.'"[5] In his homily, delivered at the Mass preceding the promulgation of *Nostra Aetate*, Paul VI said that the face of the Church had been made more beautiful through this declaration.[6] We might, entirely on the contrary, consider that starting from that day, the image of the Church, the Spouse without spot or wrinkle, holy and immaculate, the unique means of salvation, was distinctly marred, not least in the sight of her own children.

The minority became more and more aware that it had been definitively defeated. It could muster 300 votes at most; although 450 bishops signed the petition which demanded that communism be opposed by name, but which by ill luck arrived "too late," as the official reply put it, to trigger an amendment. The debates occasioned by the examination of, and the vote on, the declaration *Dignitatis Humanae* on religious freedom were nevertheless exceptionally hard-fought. Even before the opening of the Council it was known that the project was incompatible with the preceding Magisterium. When the text was first laid before the Council, during the second session, this incompatibility was even more obvious, now that its promoters had grown in self-confidence. Their adversaries, Cardinals Ottaviani, Ruffini, and Browne; Aniceto Fernandez, the Superior General of the Dominicans; Cardinals José María Bueno y Monreal of Seville and Fernando Quiroga Palacios of Santiago de Compostela; and the leading voices of *Coetus Internationalis Patrum*,

---

[4] *La Civiltà Cattolica*, editorial, October 7, 1995.

[5] Ibid., editorial, October 21, 1995.

[6] Paul VI, Homily at the Session in which three Decrees and two Declarations were promulgated, October 28, 1965.

namely Monsignor Lefebvre and Monsignor de Proença Sigaud, observed that the Church was about to consecrate the liberalism that she had been condemning for the previous two centuries. Monsignor Luigi-Maria Carli, for example, declared on September 16, 1965:

> The report of the Commission recognizes that there is a considerable distance between the teaching of Scripture and the modern doctrine of the freedom of religion within society. In order to bridge this gap, the Commission had the choice, either to condemn the modern conception or to twist the teaching of Scripture. It has chosen the latter option.... There can be no right to spread error among Catholics: there is only the choice between preventing it and tolerating it.

The Commission's relator, Monsignor De Smedt, tried to explain that the solemn condemnations issued by Gregory XVI, Pius IX, and Leo XIII, were aimed at the freedom of conscience and freedom of worship that were favored by rationalism and laicism. Above all, the supporters of religious freedom, the bishops of the United States in unison and a large section of the European bishops, supported by Monsignor Carlo Colombo, the theologian of Paul VI, were persuaded that the adoption of the text was a *sine qua non* for opening up a dialogue between the Church and the modern world.

The process common to magisterial withdrawals thus operated again, but in this case with maximum effect: the objective of opening the Church up to the world did not just lead to the omission of a condemnation, or to the masking of a traditional teaching with a new doctrine half sketched out, but led outright to the cancellation of the old and its replacement by the new. It is true that so far as dialogue with the non-Christian religions is concerned, the novel concept of paying the "respect" due to them, is as serious as allowing separated Christians to participate in the Eucharist under certain conditions. [7] In reality, this process of magisterial withdrawal in which Vatican II was engaged operated of necessity across the board: it was the intention of the assembly as a whole, laid down from the start, "not to judge," in the doctrinal sense of the term (that is to say, not to issue definitions and not to condemn), which gradually assumed a fixed form following a series of vague statements or failures to issue statements.

Nevertheless the nature of the Church is such that she cannot simply write off such deficiencies. Questions the supreme Magisterium fails to address in a timely manner become unavoidable and must be resolved: are separated Christians, in so far as they are separated, partially Catholic? Is it possible to accord respect to religious "ways" other than the Way of Christ? Can the law legitimately grant a *right*, and no longer just a *tolerance*, to what is contrary to religious truth or the moral good?

The positions for and against religious freedom were irreconcilable. The first set of modifications, which the text underwent prior to being presented again in the session of 1964, could not change any of that. In order to respond to a request of Monsignor Garrone, the text included a long historical analysis intended to justify the evolution of the Church's doctrine on this subject. But this section, which felt too much like a retrospective justification of decisions already taken, and which was quite unconvincing, was eventually suppressed. At base, it was the influence of the Jesuit John Courtney Murray, the expert attached to Cardinal Francis Spellman, Archbishop of New York, which became clearly manifest. He had not been involved in the drafting, but he was regarded as a specialist in the subject, and had been awarded, if one can use the word, a ban on publishing anything on religious freedom dating from 1955. The project became

---

[7] *Unitatis Redintegratio*, no. 8.

clearly more liberal and was based on the assumption that political authority is by nature secular and without jurisdiction in religious matters: the special civil status granted to the Church was no longer granted as standard, as the basic assumption, but might in practice arise from "particular circumstances."[8] Everything that Leo XIII, Pius XI, and Pius XII might have said on the subject, in a diametrically opposed sense, was regarded as never having come into effect. We were on a different planet.

The vote on the text should have been taken during the last week of the session, but Paul VI adjourned its definitive examination to the following session. On September 21, 1965 the text received the formal approval of Cardinal Charles Journet, of whom it was said that when he was appointed a cardinal, Jacques Maritain was elevated to the purple. Religious liberty was defined:

> This freedom means that all men are to be immune from coercion on the part of individuals or of social groups and of any human power, in such wise that no one is to be forced to act *in a manner contrary to his own beliefs, whether privately or publicly, whether alone or in association with others, within due limits*. The council further declares that the right to religious freedom has its foundation in the very dignity of the human person as this dignity is known through the revealed word of God and by reason itself. This right of the human person to religious freedom is to be recognized in the constitutional law whereby society is governed and thus it is to become a civil right.... In consequence, the right to this immunity continues to exist even in those who do not live up to their obligation of seeking the truth and adhering to it....[9]

---

[8] Second Vatican Council, Declaration *Dignitatis Humanae*, December 7, 1965, no. 6.

[9] Ibid., no. 2.

If the first part of the definition did not raise any concerns, since the Magisterium of the Church had constantly asserted that the act of faith should be freely willed, the definition's specific new contribution lay in the second part, that is to say in the right to act according to one's conscience, even if it was misdirected or in bad faith, in private as in common, as an individual or as part of a group. This was properly speaking the new right to religious freedom, as newly taught: according to *Dignitatis Humanae*, every man must be recognized as having the right, in the national community to which he belongs, to carry out public acts of worship, witness, and mission, in conformity with the religion of his choice, whether it be true or false, without the public authorities being authorized in principle ultimately to forbid the propagation of religious error. The proviso included in the words, "within due limits," even though it poses delicate problems of application—such as who will decide, and on what criteria, that a given sect has gone beyond the "limits," given that the following paragraph talks about "just public order," a restriction similar to that of the *Declaration of the Rights of Man.*[10] The proviso does not modify the substance of the affirmation at all: even if freedom is restricted by "limits," even if it is posited as the consequence of the obligation freely to seek the truth, the Council firmly lays down as a right the freedom publicly to express one's religious convictions, whether true or false.

We can make a comparison with the last papal affirmation of the traditional doctrine, that of Pius XII twelve years earlier, in his address *Ci Riesce*, which we must quote again. The ideological situation in which the Church found herself at that time was comparable in every regard to that of 1965, neither more nor less rationalist, neither

---

[10] "No one may be disquieted for his opinions, even religious ones, provided that their manifestation does not trouble the public order established by the law" (*Declaration of the Rights of Man and of the Citizen* [1789], §10).

more nor less laicist. Pius said,

> No human authority, no state, no community of states, whatever be their religious character, can give a positive command or positive authorization to teach or to do that which would be contrary to religious truth or moral good.

This principle is linked with that of tolerance:

> The duty of repressing moral and religious error cannot therefore be an ultimate norm of action. It must be subordinate to higher and more general norms, which in some circumstances permit, and even perhaps seem to indicate as the better policy, toleration of error in order to promote a greater good.[11]

We can also compare chapter 9 of the schema *De Ecclesia* prepared by the Theological Commission, which summarized previous teaching and on which the Council was going to vote:

> Just as the Civil Power considers that it is part of its duty to defend public morality, so the Civil Power is able, for the purposes of preserving citizens from the attractions of error, and of maintaining the Civil State itself in unity of belief, which is the supreme good and the fountain also of many temporal goods, to impose limits of its own accord on the public manifestations of other cults, and to defend its citizens against the spread of false doctrines which, in the opinion of the Church, put their eternal salvation at risk.... And for that reason consideration must always be given, not only to the common good of the Church, but also to the common good of the Civil State, for the sake of which a reasonable tolerance, supported also by punitive law, may

---

[11] *Ci Riesce*, no. 5.

> be imposed by the State in accordance with the circumstances of the time.[12]

The conciliar declaration proceeded therefore to what was quite simply an inversion: what had previously been regarded as a matter of *tolerance* now became a *right*.

On December 7, 1965, the last day of the Council, the declaration on religious freedom was put to the vote in the presence of Paul VI: 2,300 voted *placet*, 69 voted *non placet*. On the following day, December 8, at the solemn closing of the assembly, Paul VI symbolically placed the text in the hands of his friend Maritain. The day of the vote, December 7, had seen the publication of the Motu Proprio *Integrae Servandae* which transformed the Congregation of the Holy Office into the Congregation for the Doctrine of the Faith. "Because there is no fear in love (1 Jn 4:18)," said *Integrae Servandae* in explanation, "the defense of the faith is now better served by promoting doctrine." Thus, on the final day of the Council, the intentions that had been expressed in the opening speech were fully realized. Cardinal Ottaviani joked, "I am a general who no longer fights and who has been appointed a head teacher," and his successor, Cardinal Siri, said without obfuscation, "In the old days it was the duty of the Holy Office to defend the faith: now all that has changed."

[12] Schema *De Ecclesia*, cap. 9.5–6.

CHAPTER 10

The Council's Liturgy

VATICAN II WAS therefore a Council the like of which had never been seen in the history of the Church. Was it not to be expected that it should produce a liturgical reform that can be compared with no other? It is no exaggeration to say that this reform is a religious and cultural event without precedent in the history of the Church, and even, from certain points of view, in the liturgical history of the West. The meaning of the Catholic liturgy certainly has not changed fundamentally; on the contrary, the new liturgy has, despite very important changes, preserved numerous references to its traditions, but these references have become as it were artificial, branches grafted onto a new stock. That is substantially what the new liturgy is: the same has become different. The memory of the old has not been broken, but it is not the same type of memory. From a culture of continuity, which could accommodate multiple mutations, but which always experienced itself as diving infinitely deep into its origins ("immemorial" rites), we have moved to a memory that is reconstructed.

In reality, "liturgical services," as the constitution *Sacrosanctum Concilium* quite rightly recalled, "are not private functions, but are celebrations of the Church, which is the 'sacrament of unity,' namely, the holy people united and ordered under their bishops." That is really why the historical development of the Church's public worship is so intimately linked to that of its dogma. The liturgy, as it adapts to suit different times and different peoples, shows the understanding of Revelation developing in harmony and progressing in ways similar—the details of the analogy will need to be clarified—to those of the living Magisterium whose object is "to elucidate and explain what is contained in the deposit of faith only obscurely and implicitly."[1]

We all know the famous saying: "let us learn what we should believe from the way in which we pray; *legem credendi statuat lex supplicandi*, let the law of prayer establish the law of belief."[2] The meaning of the saying is however relatively complex. At the time of the "liturgical movement," which we have mentioned, and particularly in the 1950s, people willingly upheld the authority with which the Church's public prayer was vested as a privileged organ of tradition. Pius XII, warning us in *Mediator Dei* that the liturgy should not be seen as an area for experimentation or for verifying doctrines on the basis of the fruits that they produce or do not produce (today we would talk of "orthopraxy"), observed: it is first of all because it is subordinate to the supreme Magisterium that the prayer of the Church "fixes" the rule of faith as one of the modes in which this same Magisterium expresses itself.[3] In reality, these are two aspects of the single function of a "theological source": magisterial decisions and theological studies have constantly drawn their principles, proofs, and criteria from the formulae of prayer, the sacramental rites, and the uses of the different Churches in communion with Rome. In the hierarchy of witnesses to tradition, liturgical "monuments" stand higher even than the theology of the Fathers. It is on this basis that Vatican II affirms the sacramental character of the episcopate, the highest rank of the ecclesiastical order, by invoking "liturgical custom" and by citing a liturgical document of the ancient Church, the *Apostolic Tradition* of Hippolytus,

---

[1] *Humani Generis*, no. 21.

[2] Pope Celestine (attr.), *Letter to the Bishops of Gaul.*

[3] *Mediator Dei*, nos. 46–58.

several sacramentaries,[4] and a prayer taken from the Byzantine ordination rites.[5]

It is possible to maintain, for example, that right at the beginning Christology developed at the same time as it was being put into words at sacramental celebrations: the baptismal confessions of faith, and the proclamations of the Death and Resurrection of Christ in the breaking of bread. The history of dogma has always been inextricably linked with the history of the liturgy, or to put it better, it is one and the same history. Thus a preface was developed to give a liturgical explanation of the doctrine of the Trinity; a prayer to explain the gratuity with which God's gifts are given while explaining the necessity of asking for them; and a feast to explain a privilege of the Virgin Mary. Of course, one must not elevate the historical evolution of liturgical forms in themselves into an absolute. Strictly speaking, the impossibility of a reversal only applies to the expression of the faith and its morals: what that means is that the liturgy's role of teaching the Christian mystery cannot go back on itself. But looked at from points of view other than those of the magisterial teaching which it contains, the liturgy can contain faulty material (for example, a pious feast in honor of a vision the evidence for which does not withstand historical scrutiny). One can say, it is true, that the expression itself of the faith and of praise is relative in terms of time and space, but this relativity works in a double sense: a given form of piety can correspond to a vanished cultural sensibility, and its preservation can seem out of place. On the other hand, the obvious attachment to the tradition of the *lex orandi* by means of forms received from the past engenders a sense, which one might almost call carnal, of the immutability of the faith.

---

[4] Sacramentaries, in the days before the development of the missal, were liturgical books providing the celebrant with the prayers that he needed, i.e. the Canon and the Propers.

[5] *Lumen Gentium*, nos. 21, 26.

If therefore the last Council expressed itself in the manner of a new type of Magisterium, the liturgy which it bred ought to be the liturgical translation of that Magisterium. We will restrict ourselves here to the Mass, which by reason of its nature was most affected by the reform. It is also where the effect on Catholics as a whole was most significant. From what one might term the formal point of view (public prayer is regulated by the hierarchical Magisterium) there is no doubt that there was a departure, or what amounts to the same thing, an adaptation of Christian worship to the new mode of expression—or rather of non-expression—of the magisterial authority. In the same way, from the material point of view, we find in the new liturgy a reflection of the new doctrinal state, fuzzier and harder to grasp. Let us look at each aspect in turn.

A NEW LITURGY THAT REJECTS RITUAL

From the formal point of view, that is to say that of the demonstration of the magisterial authority's self-effacement, we would need to list all the departures from the prescribed official norms taken habitually by the majority of the leading performers in the liturgy: it is clear that the majority of celebrants interpret the rites that they perform—often with the best pastoral intentions in the world—in their own way and relative to the particular congregation. One priest breaks the host before the consecration, at the words, "He took bread . . . said the blessing, broke the bread . . ."; another prefaces the Our Father with a vigorous address; and a third piously gets the children around the altar to kiss the host. An inquisitive observer who had the time to visit a dozen churches on a Sunday to compare the celebrations would note countless variations, not only from one parish to another, but even within a single parish. Anyone who on Sunday regularly follows the Masses broadcast by the program *Le Jour de Seigneur* can without even leaving his home get an idea of the variation among the churches of France, despite the efforts of the architects of the new Mass at uniformity.

We need only remember, from this point of view, that the liturgy subsequent to Vatican II leads entirely naturally to a superabundance of commentary on what is said and done in the course of the celebrations. Bringing a ritual which is already not very distinctive down a gear moreover introduces a feeling of extreme weariness and flatness, as happens in Masses celebrated by the pious priest who comments on all the prayers and explains all the gestures: "Now the priest is going to present to God the bread obtained by the hard labor of men, Blessed are you, God of the universe, you who give us this bread..."; "All together, we proclaim our faith to the Christ who is present in the midst of us: great is the mystery of the faith . . . etc." All that is a consequence of rites in which novelty predominates (in the form of introductions and re-orderings) in comparison with rites that are handed down: the second sort of rite explains itself much better through collective sensibility and memory (though without ever excluding the necessity of catechesis), while the first type calls for supportive explanations. It turns out that the reform which followed the Council has brought about nothing less than a reworking of the whole and of all the parts of the Roman liturgy.

We must also underline that the flexible delinking—a sort of accordion effect—of the hierarchical authority and the liturgy is to be found written into the very composition of the new formulae. The liturgy to which Vatican II gave birth presents itself as intrinsically less hierarchical. This characteristic was accentuated all the more because the development of the new ritual took place in an intellectual climate that was anti-juridical, and became in effect anti-rubrical.[6] The celebrants, and in

[6] The rubrics are the instructions concerning the performance of the ceremony written in red letters, or rubrae, as part of the liturgical text.

particular the priest, are certainly central to the new rites. In one way, the distinction between the president and the faithful is accentuated, since the traditional liturgical forms were better at placing all those involved in one and the same ritualized assembly, whereas the character of the new ritual, which is in objective terms more theatrical, underlines more strongly the distinction between actors and spectators. But the personal contribution of the celebrant, his own presenter's "style" which is today greatly accentuated, is influenced by the "liturgy" of secular life: his role is not dissimilar to that of the master of ceremonies of a group event, or that of a host receiving his invited guests, in this case to a liturgical festivity, and it is less clear that he is the representative of the "teaching Church," invested with the mysterious grace of priesthood, still less that he is an *alter Christus*.

It is moreover astonishing that, even though seminarians in the old days were given courses in preaching, with practical exercises in front of a simulated "public," postulants for the priesthood today receive no general instruction in the dramatic arts adapted to the celebration of ritual. It has often been remarked, in this connection, that Paul VI had a very colorless, not to say austere, manner of celebrating his own liturgy, whereas John Paul II, benefiting from his youthful dramatic experience, found it easy to convey a very strong "presence." So far as the "ritualism" of Benedict XVI is concerned, he deliberately went against the tendency of Paul VI's liturgy, while the free and easy approach of Pope Francis has in its own way revived it again.

Moreover, the immense variability written into the new ritual itself demonstrates very clearly the weakening of its hierarchical character: unity is certainly not synonymous with uniformity, but it is much less easy to identify a thing when it shatters into a myriad of pieces. So far as concerns the essential part of the Mass, the unique Roman Canon has given place to an entire artist's palette of Eucharistic Prayers (there are today officially eleven, or fourteen if one counts as four separate Eucharistic Prayers the prayers for special circumstances, as does the missal of 2002). Each celebrant is left to interpret for himself the very brief guidance on gestures given in the rubrics. There are alternative options for the acclamations, alternatives conceived for the prayers, recommended variants for the notices and the greetings, and choices prescribed for the usage or non-usage of vestments (in any case, easily customized for particular regions).

Even more striking is the fragmented nature of the Roman rite, arising from the wide powers given to episcopal conferences to decide on a considerable number of individual norms, and above all because of the triumph of the vernacular languages.[7] If we ignore the new compositions in vernacular languages or dialects (expressly allowed for by an instruction of the Commission for the Application of the Constitution on the Sacred Liturgy), the "Latin" liturgy is celebrated in some five hundred authorized translations, which profess to be of good quality, and which despite that do not give phrase-by-phrase translations of the original text but exemplify as many different interpretations as there are regional or national styles.[8] The majority of "Roman" Catholics no longer pray in the language of Rome, not even as a testimony to their unity which could have been preserved in some parts of the Mass.

THE "FEEBLE" CONTENT OF THE NEW LITURGY

It is precisely this openness of today's liturgy to manipulation that is evidence of the unprecedented doctrinal situation inaugurated by Vatican II. This is the second aspect of the new liturgy that should be noticed, which reflects the new doctrinal state of affairs, itself quite fuzzy and difficult to grasp. There is an affinity between the flexibility

---

7 *Sacrosanctum Concilium*, no. 22.

8 Vatican Instruction *Comme le prévoit*, January 25, 1969, no. 43.

of the new *lex orandi* and the fact that the Council did not want to assume the authority of a properly dogmatic *lex*. And that is seen particularly in the content of the liturgy.

The first characteristic of the new doctrinal situation is precisely that it is new. In the conciliar *aggiornamento*, expressed by the liturgical reform, the new form is in some sense a foundational document. That is a way of saying that the rigor of the previous theological concepts has been replaced by expressions of indeterminate meaning. We neither encounter new content, which would be clearly heterodox, nor a new presentation of the same content, which would be a matter of no consequence: the very newness of the form is intended to make a statement; it is intended to be in itself an additional reason for believing. It was the task of the new liturgy to express this "intuition": the Council, at a time when the Church was engaged in refashioning the idea that she had of herself in a world that was changing at great speed and becoming more and more distant from her, wanted to show that the Church still had citizenship rights since she too was capable of changing herself. Unfortunately the world has continued to change and what was new has now aged, and not very well.

At any event, that is why the reform of the liturgy had to be so thorough-going: it was necessary to show that from now on everything in the Church would look different. Thus the conciliar texts that particularly reflected the *aggiornamento*, such as those relating to dialogue with non-Christian religions and ecumenism, were all of them responses to "the signs of the times":

> In our time, when day by day mankind is being drawn closer together, and the ties between different peoples are becoming stronger, the Church examines more closely her relationship to non-Christian religions.[9]

---

[9] *Nostra Aetate*, no. 1.

> Today, in many parts of the world, under the inspiring grace of the Holy Spirit, many efforts are being made in prayer, word, and action to attain that fullness of unity which Jesus Christ desires. The Sacred Council exhorts all the Catholic faithful to recognize the signs of the times and to take an active and intelligent part in the work of ecumenism.[10]

It may be a trite observation, but the Church was submitting herself to schooling by the world, which was teaching her things about herself. She still had to pray, even so, but in some way as directed by the profane world.

To tell the truth, the first aim of the dialogue with non-Christian religions, and of the ecumenical approach to the separated brethren, was to restore a Church without stain or wrinkle, by plunging her into the waters of the world of today: the Church does not engage in dialogue principally to prepare the way for missionary success, but to reveal herself as a Church that engages in dialogue, at the heart of a liberal world. This doctrinal renewal proceeded by setting aside any "rigidity" in what the Church had to say. At the risk of repeating ourselves, we must recall that the correct understanding of the conciliar intuitions is neither progressivist nor conservative. Ecumenism only retains its full interest—and to be frank, the existence that it would lose if it were merged either in a clearly heterodox position or in traditional doctrine—to the extent that it is not confronted with the problematic notion of "return." To put it another way, ecumenical dialogue, understood in accordance with "the spirit of the council," finds its completion in remaining incomplete (something that its results, sixty years after the Council, tend to confirm: absence of a reunion and what is approaching an additional split).

In the same way, what the reforms of Vatican II hoped to create was a liturgy that would neither be exactly the same

---

10 *Unitatis Redintegratio*, no. 4.

(there was no question of restricting change to a classic restoration as had occurred in the history of the Roman rite) nor entirely different (something that would have amounted to the Protestant desacralization with which the new rite has often been charged and which it manages to achieve in its countless "abuses"). The liturgy had to clothe itself, as did the teaching of doctrine, in a new presentation that went beyond the merely formal but stopped short of fundamental change. In other words, the purpose of the reform was essentially to indicate a readiness to reform.

The symbol of the new liturgy's character that makes the most immediate impact, even more than the abandonment of Latin, which in its way powerfully contributes to the creation of a commonplace effect, is the displacement of the altar. Archaeologists argue endlessly about the different positions occupied by the altar in the primitive basilicas. It is certain, at least, that the problematic notion of celebrating "facing the people" was completely unknown: if the altar was, in fact, in certain cases, placed facing the people, that was either so that it was oriented, that is turned to face the East, or for other liturgical reasons (such as the presence of an enclosure restricted to the clergy behind the altar), but certainly not so that the celebrant should face the congregation.

Today, celebration "facing the people" is insisted upon and indicates the break with "immemorial" custom that has taken place. Every visitor to a church, whether he enters a cathedral or a country chapel where the liturgy is only occasionally celebrated, immediately finds himself faced with two altars, the old and the new, or even a new altar and an empty space where the old was. This visual impression is moreover what one receives first, even if it is not analyzed intellectually because the lines and the atmosphere of a traditional sacred building at once focus the eye on the high altar. But in front of this high altar, or the place which it used to occupy, there is a second altar whose upsetting effect on the visual perspective is increased by the fact that it is made to be more prominent. Even if it is placed on a raised dais, this new altar is generally lower, more like a table, and brought closer to the faithful if not actually placed in their midst. After the passage of some years, and under pressure from those who administer the country's historical monuments, this altar has sometimes been of some artistic merit, or has even been assembled out of antique constituents, a Louis XV credence table, or a small tomb-altar stripped of its accompanying framework. But it is still a new altar (in the world of symbolism, the old altar was often preserved, consciously or not, to make the change clear).

The entire liturgy is formed of symbols that take part in its role of mediation. We could say that the new presentation of the official prayer of the Church has tended to give it a sociological dressing. One of the aspects of the theological crisis of the 1950s and 1960s was the confrontation with the human sciences. In the liturgy the phenomenon took the form of the feeling that there was an urgent necessity to link up with "worldly realities." This produced a new note in the explanations that were given of symbolism: the secularized "sign of the peace"—a handshake, an embrace—that is exchanged, sometimes at a distance, by the participants is intended to show their brotherly friendship and their solidarity; the "benedictions" which replace the offertory underline the significance of the bread and wine as "fruit of the earth and work of human hands."

The theme of "active participation" is not unrelated to this process: the clergy of the 1960s dreamed and talked only about *vie en équipes* (team living) and *pastorale d'ensemble* (ministry to the assembly). But the fundamental point, which was of wider application than participation, was that the remodeled liturgy had to be more explicit, more easily understood by contemporary man. The theme of the liturgy as the most transparent form of pedagogy dominates the constitution *Sacrosanctum Concilium*. The conciliar Fathers had not taken thought for the fact that every exposure to analysis of a traditional ritual language in fact weakens it: emphasizing its meaning by methods of interpretation (simplification, incorporation of explanations into the rite, suppression of symbols that are thought incapable of being understood) largely removes its capacity to provide a way of approaching the mystery. A ritual language that is too expressive ceases to "express."

In accordance with the principles of *Sacrosanctum Concilium*, the revisers introduced simplifications and suppressed the repetitions, the exuberant multiplication of gestures and phrases in which sacred language delights. They proceeded to increase the quantity of readings, to insert numerous explanatory phrases, and to translate into the vernacular. We could legitimately harbor more than mere doubts about whether this improved the comprehension of the faithful. And all the more so, insofar as at the same time, intending to "go back to the sources," they weakened the "medieval" or "Tridentine" signs of adoration of the Blessed Sacrament, which formed an instructional corpus that was particularly effective at reaching our feelings (for example, they suppressed numerous genuflections, they consigned to the past Communion on the knees, they introduced and then made routine Communion in the hand, they abandoned marks of respect to, and processions with, the Blessed Sacrament, and they paid minimal attention to reservation of the Sacrament, even if all these acts of piety have today tended to reappear). Our access to the mysteries is not improved by the use of vernacular and by celebrations facing the people. True understanding is to be found much more in the fact that the signs used, ritually transfigured to signify the sacred mysteries, serve in their turn to transfigure the soul of the worshipper who sees them as purveyors of grace.

But in making these criticisms we overlook the purpose of the reform, according to which the new liturgy was to "give a signal" to contemporary man. The reformers even derived a justification from the attacks which were immediately directed at their work, confirmation of its innovatory character. For we should not forget that at the time there was a certain provocative element in the new theological discussion, directed by an intellectual elite against a faith that was too popular, which is reflected in the way in which the ceremonies were reconfigured. The action of erasing the supposed "over-emphasis of the sacrificial" in a certain number of prayers, symbols, and references (notably with the suppression of the prayers of the Offertory) was thus a far-reaching theological choice, and the more so to the extent that some ecumenists prompted movements in an anti-sacrificial direction that were frankly heterodox.

Today, when the most senior prelates, to explain the difficulties and lack of success that the reform has encountered, still appeal to the fact that it has not been sufficiently explained, the reason is that they have forgotten the avalanche of writings, homilies, and commentaries of every sort that overwhelmed the faithful for almost a decade after the Council. It is however correct that this was in fact insufficient, since the philosophy of the changes that were being implemented drew above all on an unresolved issue within the clergy, or rather within the clerical intellectuals. In sum, just as the priests at the time of the Council wore lay dress in order to be "closer to the people," so they urged the faithful to accept a liturgy that stepped outside tradition, and effectively many of them did step outside never to come back. Equally, the deep-seated intention of the liturgical reform was only ever understood by the committed militants, who shared the same topics of reflection and used the same forms of speech as the priests and religious of the 1960s. Paradoxically, in comparison with the old, the new liturgy is elitist.

However, that is not the only reason why the popular classes of society, and particularly the country people, deserted the churches: the reform was far from being a cultural barrier preventing their secularization. Moreover, even if the reformers were not understood because of the intellectual nature of their project, their liberal wing on the other hand was moving in line with the wish for a less forbidding religion. The famous complaint which followed the changes to the Mass, "They have changed our religion," full of indignation though it seemed to be, often also concealed a certain relief, even while it provided an alibi: since the Mass was losing its inflexibility, the rules for moral conduct (marital conduct, the Sunday obligation) could themselves also be more flexible. This was something that was following the trend for the conversion of Western societies to bourgeois values, a point on which we have to recognize the correctness of post-conciliar intuitions, even if they were suicidal from the institutional point of view.

That is why, when we consider the renovation of the liturgy, just as when we consider the specifically conciliar teachings, we must reject equally both the "erroneous understandings" (the celebrations of small informal communities in which people sit around the table in a dining room and share "the bread and the wine" or, today, the madmen who want to "enjoy the feast"), and the pious readings "in continuity with tradition" (the liturgies of Paul VI in Latin and Gregorian chant from Solesmes). The former annihilate the sacred action itself, while the latter work at cross-currents to the spirit of the liturgy. They distort the true meaning of the liturgy in a leftward direction (or in the case of the latter in a rightward direction). This is seen more particularly in the common manner of living out the present liturgy, with its characteristic reduction in the distance between worship and daily life: the female religious in lay dress leaving the lectern, where she directs the singing, in order to fetch the ciborium from the tabernacle; or a woman receiving Communion and asking for a second host which she slips into her handbag to take to a friend who has been unable to come to Mass.

The ceremonial, which retains enough ritual to remain a ceremony, thus constantly finds its hieratic character contradicted: the faithful form a singing procession in order to go and receive Communion, but the hosts are distributed into the hand by lay people wearing ordinary town clothes; the celebrant's vestments are as long as they were in the old days, but he continues to wear them after the Mass all through the cheery "Sunday Catholic" interchanges at the church door. The process has two halves: the traditional ritual aspect (Communion, sacred vestments) is in part made commonplace, at the same time as gestures associated with daily life (putting a piece of bread in one's mouth, chatting at the end of a meeting) are partially ritualized, with the totality generally following the cultural model of bourgeois politeness. If today there has been a certain return of a hieratic character, this is because post-conciliar enthusiasm had really gone too far in reducing the difference between the sacred and the commonplace. There must be some sort of break with the latter if there is to be any ritual left, and *a fortiori* if one is to have any sense of "making accessible": more than fifty years after the reform, the memory of the previous liturgies, which to begin with played a key role in creating the feeling that there was now a closer connection with people's everyday lives, has faded away, and the feeling of a liturgy that is being made more everyday has to be revived within the celebrations themselves.

The failure is clear, since this convergence hardly touches the reality of contemporary man, who for the most part, in the West, has no use for the prayer of the Church, to whose superficial modernity he accords at the most a polite approval. That is, if he does not lament the disfiguring of a vast cultural inheritance. So far as the faithful are concerned, does the new state of liturgical affairs lead them to a greater fervor and to a more intense communion in the mysteries of grace? A remark and a question that are pointless: it no more helps to highlight the incapacity of the liturgical revolution to promote religious practice and a knowledge of the truths of the faith, than it does to underline the fact that all the occasions of dialogue with non-Christian religions have done nothing for the missionary spirit of Catholics.

Without doubt, Paul VI had not anticipated the extent of the liturgical reform's destructive effects and the reactions in both directions (refusal, abuse) that they were bound to provoke. It was for a long time fashionable to regret the rapidity with which the changes were introduced, and to float the idea that the difficulties could have been avoided if the reformers had acted with greater prudence. In fact, even if the authoritarian manner and the speed of the reforms played a part, it was not their influence that played the greatest part in creating the effect of an earthquake. It is perhaps even possible that it was the overly lengthy spinning out of the reforms, from 1964 (the Mass facing the people with numerous vernacular sections) to 1974 (a new rite for Confession), during which easings were followed by suppressions, and simplifications by abandonments, which gave the Catholics of the period the impression of changes that would never cease. In any case, the reform introduced by the Council was inevitably so disruptive of established practices that it gave the impression that the Church had moved into a different epoch, because that was after all precisely the effect that was intended.

Innovations can of course become habitual practices, but they nevertheless keep their dynamic characteristic of being "adaptations to our time." If, following on a usage that first took root in France, priests were today to halt Communion in the hand in their parishes, it is obvious that they would not be taken for innovators targeting a "traditional" practice, but quite the opposite: this is therefore because the practice concerned has not become a tradition, on the contrary. To take an opposite example: white First Communion robes were only introduced into all the parishes of France at the very end of the 1950s or at the start of the 1960s, to replace brassards and tulle dresses. Barely ante-conciliar, and in some cases contemporary with the first reforms, they almost immediately became traditional and even became transformed into a symbol of popular tradition. The parish priests who tried, post-Vatican II, to suppress them a mere ten years after their first appearance, and replace them with "Festivals of Faith" in ordinary dress, had that brought home to them. All this points to the existence as a reference point of a living conservatory of traditions, formed subsequently to the Council by the various traditional movements. Though they were not of great numerical importance, these traditional Masses were more or less known to practicing Catholics, who unlike the clergy have always generally admitted the possibility of the existence, according to one's taste, of a diversified range of celebrations, and who themselves do not hesitate to attend different types of celebration according to the occasion. The resemblance of the tradition to the statue of the Commander has always come, and comes even more so today, from the fact of the decline in parish Mass attendance contrasted with the enduring numbers of those faithful to the traditional Mass, present at the back of the conciliar stage.[11] We could even ask whether this tension is not necessary for the Church to be truly conciliar.

We deceive ourselves therefore if we talk about the long time that has always been required for the reception of councils and reforms. We are mistaken if we believe that

---

[11] The "statue of the Commander" has become proverbial, at any rate in France, for a defeated and disregarded enemy who reappears from the shadows to destroy his former adversary. The phrase takes its origin from the story of Don Juan, the famous Spanish libertine. After trying to seduce the daughter of the Commander of Seville, he kills the Commander in a duel. Subsequently, encountering a statue of the Commander in a graveyard, Don Juan invites it to dinner. To Don Juan's surprise, the statue appears at the appointed time, seizes him, and drags him off to hell.

the tension created by the new liturgy can be eased: the tension is built into the liturgy. The faithful have now long been habituated to the liturgy of Paul VI, but it will never become tradition. People can like or not like the tone of the following consecratory prayers, childish and redolent of daily life as they are, but will never get a sense, as they listen to them, that the prayers are a link in a chain going back to times immemorial:

> Most holy Father, we would like to show you our gratitude. We have brought this bread and this wine: may they become for us the body and blood of the risen Jesus. Then we will be able to offer to you what comes from you. One evening, in truth, just before his death, Jesus was eating with his apostles. He took some of the bread from the table. In his prayer, he dedicated it to you. Then he shared out the bread, while saying to his friends, Take, and eat it, all of you: this is my body which given up for you.[12]

The example of this text may not seem conclusive: but this composition, placed at the heart of the sacred synaxis to express the greatest of all liturgical mysteries, is remarkable precisely because of its almost touching insipidity. Its lack of syntactic subordination, its exceptionally condescending focus on ordinary life—a real *kenosis* in the midst of the commonplace—perfectly captures the conciliar reform of the Roman liturgy. With the doors and windows wide open to admit the most extreme spiritual drought, it is really the most expressive theological statement of the conciliar message.

---

[12] Père très saint, nous voudrions te montrer notre reconnaissance. Nous avons apporté ce pain et ce vin, qu'ils deviennent pour nous le corps et le sang de Jésus ressuscité. Alors nous pourrons t'offrir ce qui vient de toi. Un soir, en effet, juste avant sa mort, Jésus mangeait avec ses Apôtres. Il prit du pain sur la table. Dans sa prière, il t'a béni. Puis il a partagé le pain, en disant à ses amis, Prenez, et mangez-en tous, ceci est mon corps livré pour vous (Masses with Children, First Eucharistic Prayer).

CHAPTER 11

The Battle over the Mass

ENTHUSIASM FOR THE liturgical reform evaporated long ago. The experts have departed (the last survivors, Pierre-Marie Gy, Pierre Jounel, and Louis Bouyer, all died in 2004). The most militant priests of the early days have also departed, for the most part, with a good number having earlier left the priesthood. The Tridentine liturgy celebrated by the priests ordained by Monsignor Lefebvre, or with full official approval by the communities recognized by John Paul II in *Ecclesia Dei*, or again by diocesan priests in their parishes, and also in the monasteries, continues to provide competition, which is all the stronger given that, proportionate to the numbers of faithful involved, it is the communities celebrating this liturgy which attract the most vocations.[1]

The post-conciliar climate has vanished from memory. A certain number of bishops and senior churchmen, appointed since the 1980s, had tried, in the rather unacademic words of Cardinal Jean-Marie Lustiger, to "blow the whistle marking the end of play-time." During the period of the apparent Wojtylian reconquest, at least at the start of it, they thought that they could recover for Catholicism a certain right to exist on the basis of "religious demand," which is in fact a phenomenon of extreme individualism. But everything suggests that after the end of the pontificate of Paul VI, everyone was playing

[1] The Tridentine liturgy is that promulgated in the Missal mandated by the Council of Trent in 1570. This Missal was intended to put an end to the variations in the Mass which had come into existence between different dioceses and religious orders, but the Council of Trent nevertheless allowed the continuation of any rite that could show that it had been in use for 200 years or more.

it by ear, trying for as long as possible to avoid searing examinations of conscience.

In reality, the majority of today's celebrations reflect an image of disenchantment: lassitude, boredom sometimes, and always mediocrity. Even if we omit the unavoidable ageing of the sacerdotal body, everyone knows it and the poverty of the new liturgy says it out aloud: the sap is rising elsewhere. Real freshness is to be found in the sumptuous oriental liturgies, in the liturgies reinfused with a heavy dose of tradition, or even outside the sanctuary in the astonishing revival of interest in medieval chant and in Baroque choral music, in what we might term reculturation, which takes place in addition to or in opposition to the official liturgy and permanently discredits it. It makes no difference that the new liturgy clings to the ideological phenomenon which is the "spirit of the Council," and maintains itself and will maintain itself as such, despite every evidence of failure, until such time as second thoughts are permitted.

The deficiencies of the new rite are so obvious that its critics, in failing to challenge the principles behind it, have been as ineffective as they have been numerous, and that includes those at the most senior level. The collapse of our patrimony of the Latin liturgy in so short a time, this immense moral rupture, constitutes one of the most troubling features of the story of the contemporary Church. One day it will be necessary to draw up an account of the sacred vessels, the ornaments, and the works of art consigned to the jumble sales, a loss which accompanied the massacre of the liturgical patrimony and was very real and lucrative for those who benefited from it. And we should expect that future generations, whatever opinions they bring to the table, will lay the blame on those Catholic leaders who presided over a cultural and pastoral disaster without precedent. In any case, the powerful stream of apologetic which emanated from the Catholic Church at the time of the liturgical movement right up until the 1960s (we should think of the witness of Edith Stein, Julien Green, Max Jacob, Marie Noël, Jacques Maritain, and of so many others) has not only vanished, but has even gone into reverse.

The deficiencies of the reform were pointed out from the start. In a context in which doctrinal expressions were relativized, many aspects of the new liturgy immediately appeared very worrying. Of course, each of the modifications introduced could be justified if taken on its own. But the accumulation of the changes, in a very specific theological context, could only generate alarm: the reform took place in the presence of Protestant observers, in an ecumenical context that was incomprehensible from a doctrinal point of view, and even formed part of this ecumenical process. Thus the weakening—and how easy it is to perceive it—of everything related to the Real Presence could only be deeply troubling, just like the diminution of the hierarchical aspect of the liturgy, whose unchanging nature was part and parcel of its status of official prayer, which was replaced by a mode of expression that was changeable and to an important extent handed over to individual creativity.

The most obvious, for those whose senses were alerted to this doctrinal contraction, was the fact that the *Novus Ordo Missae* expressed less clearly than its predecessor the fact that the Mass is a propitiatory sacrifice (a sacrifice offered for our sins), renewing the redemptive sacrifice of the Cross. We should note that at the time of the reform this idea of a "sacrifice for sin" was being "re-evaluated." Criticism of the theology of propitiatory sacrifice and of the vicarious sacrifice (Christ taking the sins of mankind onto himself to make reparation on mankind's behalf) was at the time very fashionable. The criticism, moreover, did not lack valid arguments when it focused on certain over-simplistic formulations. Current, however, were criticisms like those of Hans Küng, who was not at that time thought of as an extremist:

> The theology of the Counter-Reformation has paid the price, where its teaching on the Eucharist was concerned, of many biases which give cause for concern: the abandonment of the commemorative aspect, on which much emphasis was still placed in the Middle Ages, in just the same way as the communion aspect was in the other direction focused on the sacrificial aspect. Now, it is exactly the notion of sacrifice and the way in which it is made actual, that pose numerous questions which still lack answers.[2]

The new missal thus gave every sign that it was proceeding along these lines, diverting the focus that the liturgy of the Mass had previously placed on the sacrifice of Good Friday (the blood shed for us) in the direction of the Paschal Mystery in its entirety. That was very clear, for example, in the acclamations that were added to the consecration rite and which defined the "mystery of the faith" which had just been accomplished, not as the renewal of the oblation of Calvary, but as the proclamation all together and at one moment of "the Death," "the Resurrection," and the "coming again" in glory of Jesus Christ. Certainly, an affirmation of the truth, but one that erases the primordial aspect of the renewal of the act of the Cross: the Body that was given, the Blood that was shed. It was no longer a requirement that a crucifix should be placed in the center of the altar to dominate the celebration of the sacrifice. An impressive number of propitiatory prayers was removed:

> Take away from us our iniquities . . . O Lord . . . , that thou wouldst vouchsafe to forgive me all my sins . . . , deliver me by this thy most holy Body and Blood from all my iniquities . . . , that

[2] Hans Küng, *Kirche im Konzil* (Freiburg im Breisgau: Herder, 1963), French trans. by Maurice Barth, *Le Concile, épreuve de l'Église* (Paris: Éditions du Seuil, 1963).

> no stain of sin may remain in me..., that the sacrifice ... may be acceptable to thee....[3]

The most substantial reduction was the suppression of the traditional offertory, replaced by a "presentation of the gifts." There is no doubt that the reformers targeted the tone of the offertory and its accumulation of sacrificial prayers:

> Receive, O holy Father, almighty, eternal God, this spotless host, which I, thy unworthy servant, do offer unto thee, my living and true God, for mine own countless sins, offences, and omissions.... We offer unto thee, O Lord, the chalice of salvation.... In an humble spirit, and a contrite heart, may we be received by thee, O Lord; and may our sacrifice so be offered up in thy sight this day that it may be pleasing to thee.... Receive, O holy Trinity, this offering, which we make to thee, in remembrance of the Passion, Resurrection, and Ascension.... Brethren, pray that my sacrifice and yours may be acceptable to God the Father Almighty.[4]

Already in 1952, Joseph A. Jungmann, in his *Missarum Sollemnia*, had urged that the offertory formed "a certain duplication" of the prayers of the Canon, something that

---

[3] Aufer a nobis, quaesumus Domine, iniquitates nostras ... ut indulgere digneris omnia peccata mea ... libera me per hoc sacrosanctum corpus et sanguinem tuum ab omnibus iniquitatibus meis ... ut in me non remaneat scelerum macula ... ut sacrificium ... tibi sit acceptabile....

[4] Suscipe, sancte Pater, omnipotens aeterne Deus, hanc immaculatam hostiam, quam ego indignus famulus tuus offero tibi Deo meo vivo et vero, pro innumerabilibus peccatis, offensionibus et negligentiis meis.... Offerimus tibi, Domine, calicem salutaris.... In spiritu humilitatis, et in animo contrito suscipiamur a te, Domine: et sic fiat sacrificium nostrum in conspectu tuo hodie, ut placeat tibi, Domine Deus.... Suscipe, sancta Trinitas, hanc oblationem, quam tibi offerimus ob memoriam Passionis, Resurrectionis, et Ascensionis.... Orate, fratres, ut meum ac vestrum sacrificium acceptabile fiat apud Deum patrem omnipotentem.

at the time of the reform became the great justification for its suppression.[5] In reality, the liturgists could not ignore the fact that a sacramental celebration is a whole, in which we cannot make an artificial separation between the "essential" and the "accessory." Each part of the Mass is at one and the same time what it is on its own and what it represents as a meaningful part of the whole. The Communion is also both "sacrifice" and "offering," insofar as the communicants themselves become "hosts" in uniting themselves to the Body and Blood of Christ. And if the offertory is already "consecration" by virtue of the offering of the oblations (the bread and the wine), the consecration itself is essentially Jesus Christ's renewed "offering" of himself to his Father, of if you prefer, the perfect "presentation."

Moreover, everyone knows perfectly well that in all the Eastern liturgies the unity of action of the Masses and of the other celebrations is even more marked than it is in the Latin liturgies. Thus, in the ordination ceremonies of the Eastern liturgies, it is not possible to define precisely which words of the consecratory formula confer the priesthood or the episcopate. So far as the oblations of the Mass are concerned, they are honored before the recitation of the Institution as if they were already consecrated (with procession, censings, and sacrificial prayers), and conversely the celebrant asks during the prayer of the *epiclesis*, which comes after the words of the Institution, that through the action of the Holy Spirit the bread and the wine should become the Body and Blood of Christ, as if that had not already been accomplished. Who would be so rash as to speak of "doublets"? In reality, the criticism of "doublets," when faced with the venerable offertory

[5] Josef Andreas Jungmann, *Missarum Sollemnia: Eine Genetische Erklärung der Römischen Messe* (Wien: Herder, 1948), French trans. *"Missarum Sollemnia," explication génétique de la messe romaine*, 2 vols. (Paris: Aubier, 1951–52), English trans. by Francis A. Brunner, *The Mass of the Roman Rite: Its Origins and Development*, 2 vols. (New York: Benziger, 1951–55).

of the Latin liturgies, was the mark of a Cartesianism far removed from the spirit of the liturgy.

What is more, the final fault for the professor-reformers was that the prayers to be suppressed were for the most part drawn from the category of medieval prayers known as "apologies," in the sense of requests for justification, confessions of unworthiness. This type of liturgical prayer is found from the seventh century onward. They became very common in the sacramentaries from the Carolingian period onward, and reached their greatest development in the tenth and eleventh centuries. Their "flowery" style is not unlike, in a different field, the liturgical chant of the same period, in the form with which learned restorations have allowed us to become acquainted.

Each reformer had his own learned obsession. Dom Botte, whose specialty was the *Apostolic Tradition* of Hippolytus, insisted that it should be the basis for one of the Eucharistic Prayers and for the formula for ordaining bishops. Louis Bouyer, on the other hand, wanted to recover the continuity between the Eucharist and Jewish ritual meals. The apologies were therefore replaced with euchologies composed on the model of blessings from Jewish liturgical tradition. The new formulae were inspired by the evidence from the *Mishnah* for the blessings of the initial cup and of the breaking of bread during Jewish ceremonial meals. Today we know that the euchologies concerned are much later than was thought in the 1960s, and it is not impossible that some of the apologies are of similar or greater antiquity.

However that may be, the "presentation of gifts" is formulated thus in the French-language missal: when the priest raises the paten above the altar, he says, "Blessed are you, God of the universe, you who give us this bread, fruit of the earth and of the work of men; we present it to you: it will become the bread of life," instead of, "Receive, O holy Father, almighty, eternal God, this spotless host, which I, thy unworthy servant, do offer unto thee, my living and true God, for mine own countless sins, offences, and omissions."[6]

When the priest raises the chalice, he says, "Blessed are you, God of the universe, you who give us this wine, fruit of the vine and of the work of men; we present it to you: it will become the wine of the eternal Kingdom," instead of, "We offer unto thee, O Lord, the chalice of salvation, beseeching thy clemency, that it may rise up in the sight of thy divine majesty, as a savor of sweetness, for our salvation, and for that of the whole world."[7]

The prayer *In spiritu humilitatis*, "In an humble spirit, and a contrite heart, may we be received by thee, O Lord, and may our sacrifice so be offered up in thy sight this day that it may be pleasing to thee," becomes, "Humble and poor, we beg you, Lord, receive us: may our sacrifice today find grace in your presence."[8]

It is true that the prayer *Orate fratres* had been preserved at the wish of Paul VI, to the great consternation of the reformers, and that the French version was brought closer to the original in 2021: "Pray, brothers and sisters, that my sacrifice, and yours, may be acceptable to God, the almighty Father," to which the faithful reply, "May the Lord accept this sacrifice at your hands for the praise

---

[6] "Tu es béni, Dieu de l'univers, toi qui nous donnes ce pain, fruit de la terre et du travail des hommes; nous te le présentons, il deviendra le pain de la vie," instead of "Suscipe, sancte Pater, omnipotens aeterne Deus, hanc immaculatam hostiam, quam ego indignus famulus tuus offero tibi Deo meo vivo et vero, pro innumerabilibus peccatis, offensionibus et negligentiis meis."

[7] "Tu es béni, Dieu de l'univers, toi qui nous donnes ce vin, fruit de la vigne et du travail des hommes; nous te le présentons, il deviendra le vin du Royaume éternel," instead of "Offerimus tibi, Domine, calicem salutaris, tuam deprecantes clementiam: ut in conspectu divinae Maiestatis tuae pro nostra et totius mundi salute cum odore suavitatis ascendat."

[8] "In spiritu humilitatis, et in animo contrito suscipiamur a te, Domine: et sic fiat sacrificium nostrum in conspectu tuo hodie, ut placeat tibi, Domine Deus," became "Humbles et pauvres, nous te supplions, Seigneur, accueille-nous, que notre sacrifice, ce jour, trouve grâce devant toi."

and glory of his name, for our good and the good of all the Church."[9]

But in total, could the liturgy have been made less sacrificial, and above all could it have been made even more radically new? Now, even if, up to a certain point, successive Christian generations think that they are repeating certain ceremonies identically more than they actually are doing, this urge and this feeling that we are repeating the same action are the basis of the entire Christian liturgy: "Do this in remembrance of me.... For as often as you eat this bread and drink the chalice, you proclaim the Lord's death until he comes" (1 Cor 11:24–26). Formed of actions and words that convey meaning, this continuity has to be felt, as it were physically. The failure of the reworking of the Latin liturgy, therefore, can be explained by all sorts of reasons: the intellectualism directing the project, combined with the determination on the ground to take things to extremes; the clumsy haste and the all-embracing character of a reworking that spared neither sacrament, nor office, nor blessing; or indeed a militant belief in "participation"; or again the poverty of inspiration in matters aesthetic or symbolic; etc. It remains true, beyond all the pastoral and theological failures, that the main reason behind the failure was that the reformers wanted their work to be seen as an innovation that would express "the Church's new look." The main message that they wished to convey was that the Church knew how to give herself a face-lift: that was the cause of the more than unsatisfactory reception accorded to the reworked liturgy, since nothing is more contrary to the spirit of liturgy.

As we have already said, the leading actors have ever since repeated *ad infinitum* that the changes "have not

[9] P. Priez, frères et soeurs, que mon sacrifice, et le vôtre, soit agréable à Dieu le Père tout-puissant. R. Que le Seigneur reçoive de vos mains ce sacrifice à la louange et à la gloire de son nom, pour notre bien et celui de toute l'Église.

been sufficiently explained." The opposite is true: written and oral explanations of the changes have been issued to a point of saturation. They are an integral part of the reform, which has to celebrate its own newness. And that is really why the anticipated fruits of the reform have never seen the light of day: asking the faithful, among others, to adopt formulations that reversed the work of fourteen or fifteen centuries, when these formulations were not inventions pure and simple, made it strictly impossible to perceive the thread of continuity within the prayer that makes present the continuity of belief. That was the cause of the reactions, muffled or tumultuous, to the imposition of the new liturgy.

It was on January 29, 1964, that Paul VI created a Commission for the Implementation of the Constitution on the Sacred Liturgy. The majority of the participants were experts (to the number of two hundred and fifty) who had participated directly or indirectly in the preparation of the text on which the Council had voted. The other participants were cardinals or bishops. Of course, there is no question of belittling the technical expertise of these specialists. We should even admit that it is in part thanks to the stimulation of the reform that quite remarkable historical studies have been undertaken, which contributed moreover at a later stage to undermining the categorical character of the postulates which dominated the reformers' compositions, notably the principle of celebration "facing the people." The true cause, however, is the fact that these specialists, historians of liturgy though they were, appointed themselves as creators of liturgy. We should observe at this point that until a fairly recent date liturgical science remained a subject for ecclesiastics. The closed community at the heart of the clerical world, cut off socially, as we must admit, in which the liturgical studies of the 1950s and 1960s developed, is a partial explanation of the militantly clerical attitude that the reformers generally displayed. That also enables us to understand the reformers' astonishing aesthetic and cultural insensibility to the unprecedented catastrophe that the reform represented.

Starting with the session of October 1966, five, and then six, Protestants took part in the meetings of the Commission. Paul VI appointed as its president the candidate of the left wing at the 1963 conclave, Cardinal Giacomo Lercaro (who remained at the head of the Commission until 1968, and was then replaced by Cardinal Benno Gut, the former Abbot Primate of the Benedictines). The Commission, which duplicated the role of the Congregation of Rites, disappeared with it on May 8, 1969, when a restructuring of the dicasteries created a Congregation for Divine Worship, of which Monsignor Bugnini became Secretary and Cardinal Gut the Prefect.

The Secretary designate at that time was the Lazarist Annibale Bugnini, who had been Secretary of the Commission instituted by Pius XII in 1948 to simplify the rubrics and, in 1955, to reform the provision for Holy Week. John XXIII had nominated him in 1959 as Secretary of the Commission charged with preparing the schema for the conciliar Constitution on the Sacred Liturgy. But Cardinal Lercaro, it has been said, had dismissed him from the Commission. His return therefore evened out the score. He was considered by his colleagues as rather a moderate in comparison with the party represented by Aimé-Georges Martimort, professor at the Catholic Institute of Toulouse, and more generally in comparison with the French, who exercised a real hegemony in the preparatory commission insofar as concerned the working out of grand theoretical principles. Bugnini, a dedicated worker and highly skilled at negotiations within the workings of the ecclesiastical administration, became the kingpin of the reform. In addition to that, his enthusiasm, with its lyrical touch, perfectly matched the highly romantic keenness for innovation which inspired Paul VI in the years following the Council.

For the reform of the liturgy was above all directed by Paul VI, in the same way in which he had directed the last three sessions of the Council. He followed, step by step and in the greatest detail, the working out of the transformation, formulating proposals, suggesting corrections, without however imposing all his opinions: there were even frequent negotiations between him and the experts, often resulting in a compromise. The reform which he undertook was total. Nothing escaped his attention. This is another feature which makes the reform unique in the history of the Church: it embraced the entirety of the liturgical texts, the missal, the breviary, the ritual, the pontifical, and the ceremonial of bishops, all the Latin rites without exception (the Ambrosian, the Carthusian, etc., and even the Mozarabic missal, which is no longer in daily use other than in a chapel of Toledo Cathedral!), and did not neglect to take in hand again, to modify, and to remodel, right down to the least significant ritual blessing.

To follow the reform of the Mass, we must remind ourselves that a series of preparatory changes had given priests and the faithful the impression that they had entered an era of continuous change. It would be tiresome to list the incessant modifications which were issued, either as authorizations, or as obligatory instructions, or even for experimental purposes, following the Motu Proprio *Sacram Liturgiam* of January 25, 1964, not to mention the succession of episcopal conferences. The French bishops' conference authorized the use of French for all of the Liturgy of the Word in 1964, and for the Canon in 1967, notwithstanding the fact that instructions and decrees from Rome succeeded each other, continually upsetting the habits of the faithful: April 25 and September 26, 1967, January 27 and March 7, 1965, April 17, and May 27, 1967, etc.

The changes accompanied alterations which the proponents of reform, following the end of the first session of the Council, had authorized with ever-increasing abandon and of their own accord. There was an explosion of initiatives emanating from college chaplains and from *Action Catholique*, from vicars and curés intent on creating shock starting in May 1968—we could even say from 1965, in certain dioceses, where the bishops found it necessary to remind everyone that the eucharistic fast had not been abolished. The liturgical confusion, a revolution in which one could engage at little cost, enabled entire bodies of the clergy (priests, seminarians, and militant laymen immersed in the preoccupations of the clergy) to convince themselves that a fundamental transformation was in process intended at the same time to bring the Church into line with contemporary culture and to "change the mentality" of practicing Catholics. We must never lose sight of the fact that the reform was promulgated in this atmosphere, with which it was inseparably linked from the beginning. It was this liturgy, resented as being desacralized (the vernacular introduced in heavy doses all of a sudden, the altar turned to face the people, and an infinity of other variations), which represented for the faithful the practical spread of the "Spirit of the Council." Senior Catholics were caught in a pincer between the professors, who at the head of the process trimmed and wove into new patterns texts and ceremonies that were anchored in the memory, and the militant clergy on the ground, who took advantage of the situation to turn everything upside down and often to break everything up.

Paul VI himself was able to observe the reactions which the reform produced, when he personally witnessed a demonstration of rejection. While he was celebrating the Mass in Italian, on Christmas Eve in 1966, in Florence Cathedral, he heard the deep and powerful voice of the novelist Tito Casini respond in Latin from the depths of the congregation. Casini was about to publish *La tunica stracciata*, a book which attacked the Italian Mass and which took Cardinal Lercaro violently to task, describing him as nothing less than "a new Luther."[10]

While this was going on, Bugnini speeded up the work of the Commission as much as he could, with the result that in April 1967, at its eighth plenary session, three new Eucharistic Prayers had already been drawn up. On October 24, 1967, at the meeting of the Synod of Bishops, Bugnini celebrated before the Fathers a *missa normativa* in the Sistine Chapel, with a cast of seminarians present to reproduce the atmosphere of an Italian parish. He could at once himself see the disquiet among the Fathers: "The greater part of them left the Sistine in a prejudiced and ill-disposed attitude.... The change seemed to them to be too radical." When the bishops assembled in the Synod were asked if they approved the new Mass 71 replied *placet*, 43 *non placet*, and 62 *placet juxta modum* (with reservations).

Faced with this relative lack of success, Paul VI arranged for three celebrations of the new Mass in his presence, himself presided over round-table discussions, gave and received advice, arranged for some modifications to be made, and ordered that despite everything the project should press on resolutely. Promulgated by Paul VI's constitution *Missale Romanum* of April 3, 1969, the new missal entered service on November 30, 1969, the first Sunday of Advent. Each bishops' conference was required to fix the date from which use of the new missal would be obligatory, in any case no later than November 28, 1971. The *editio typica*, or standard edition, was promulgated by a decree of the Congregation for Divine Worship of March 26, 1970, with a second *editio typica* of March 27, 1975, incorporating the abolition of the subdiaconate and introducing some changes in detail (a third *editio typica* came in 2002, with very minor changes,

---

[10] Tito Casini, *La Tunica Stracciata. Lettera Di Un Cattolico Sulla "Riforma Liturgica,"* Preface by Cardinal Antonio Bacci (Rome: Sates, 1967); English trans., *The Torn Tunic: Letter of a Catholic on the "Liturgical Reform"* (Chulmleigh: Britons, 1971; repr. Angelico Press, 2020).

apart from the happy reappearance of the word *âme*, or "soul," in a certain number of prayers or prefaces for the departed).[11]

The documents of the episcopal conferences dealing with matters that fell within their competence proliferated: use of the vernacular, provisional translations, national editions of the various books, adaptations, approvals of experiments. The French translation of the different parts of the missal, already largely in use since 1964, was definitively confirmed by a series of decrees from the same Congregation, of which the first was dated September 29, 1969. In reality, in a classic development, the regulatory avalanche led to a universal disregard for regulations, with unauthorized experiments extending as far as the improvisation of new Eucharistic Prayers, the Eucharist being celebrated in the course of a meal, etc.

Manifestations of opposition therefore began as soon as the *Novus Ordo Missae* entered into service. Cardinals Bacci and Ottaviani (the latter had resigned from his position as Prefect of the Congregation for the Doctrine of the Faith on January 6, 1968) sent Paul VI a short composition of twenty-nine pages, a *Brief Critical Examination of the New Ordo Missae*, which had in essence been edited by Father Guérard de Lauriers, a Dominican from Saulchoir. The cardinals accompanied it with a letter saying in particular,

> . . . the *Novus Ordo Missae*, if we consider the new elements susceptible to widely different interpretations which appear to be presupposed or implied, is a striking departure, both as a whole and in detail, from the Catholic theology of the Holy Mass as it was formulated in Session 22 of the Council of Trent. . . . So many innovations appear in the *Novus Ordo* and conversely so

---

[11] *Missale Romanum ex Decreto Sacrosancti Œcumenici Concilii Vaticani II Instauratum . . . Ordo Missæ*. Editio typica (Rome: Typis Polyglottis Vaticanis, 1969); *Acta Apostolicae Sedis* LXII (1970), 554.

> much that is of perennial value is relegated to a minor place or repositioned—if it still finds a place at all—that we may find reinforced or changed into a certainty the suspicion, which is alas already prevalent in many circles, that truths which have always been believed by the Christian people can be changed or passed over in silence without infidelity to the sacred deposit of doctrine to which the Catholic faith is bound in eternity.[12]

At the same time, this *Brief Examination* was made public. The expression of doubts of this sort over the orthodoxy of the new Mass emanating from Cardinal Ottaviani constituted a strong encouragement for "rebel" priests and faithful.

Paul VI, with a personal letter dated October 22, 1969, submitted the *Examination* to the Congregation for the Doctrine of the Faith. Cardinal Seper replied on November 12: "The short work contains numerous affirmations that are superficial, exaggerated, inexact, emotional, and false." Paul VI nevertheless tried to obtain a resolution in a similar way to that which he had used with the conciliar minority in order to reassure it on the subject of the doctrine of collegiality in *Lumen Gentium*, that is to say that he did not modify the actual text but published a *Preliminary Explanatory Note* which was considered to have restated the traditional doctrine. In the same way he asked for some minor changes, not to the missal itself, but to the general way in which it was presented. It was essentially no. 7 of the *Institutio Generalis Missalis Romani* which was modified.[13] Initially it declared,

---

[12] The letter is also known as the Ottaviani Intervention. See Anthony Cedaka (trans.), *The Ottaviani Intervention: Short Critical Study of the New Order of Mass* (Rockford, IL: TAN Books, 1992).

[13] The *Institutio Generalis* was printed as part of the Missal. The amendments of 1970 were published in *Notitiae* (May 1970), no. 54, 161–231. The revised *Institutio Generalis* appeared in subsequent printings of the Missal.

> The Lord's Supper or Mass is the sacred assembly or meeting of the people of God, met together with a priest presiding, to celebrate the Memorial of the Lord.

This text (which later became no. 27 in the *editio typica* of 2002), which proposed to define the mode of celebration within the chapter dedicated to the structure and elements of the Mass, sounded in reality like a doctrinal definition (which would otherwise be missing) that was at least defective. After modification it became,

> In the Mass or Lord's Supper the People of God are called together into one place where the priest presides over them and acts in the person of Christ. They assemble to celebrate the Memorial of the Lord, which is the sacrifice of the Eucharist.

The correction had the awkward result that it suggested that the first version of no. 7 was doctrinally incorrect and that it really did intend to give a doctrinal definition of the reformed Mass. The correction by its nature resembled a partial admission relating to the new liturgical content, which however remained unchanged.

The fact is that, essentially in France, the resistance to the new liturgical law reached a level which, without being considerable, was much more important than the Roman authorities had anticipated. There is not a diocese where some priests, often a dozen, more in certain cases, have not continued to celebrate the Tridentine Mass for the faithful who do not accept the reform. Their number has never diminished (something that implies a significant increase in relative terms, given the drop in the number of priests), with the older priests being succeeded by newly ordained priests from Monsignor Lefebvre's International Priestly Fraternity of Saint Pius X , or from other traditional communities. The number of the faithful who practice habitually or frequently according to the Tridentine liturgy is difficult to establish other than by occasional polls, which seem to prove that there was a notable increase at the end of the 1970s, followed by a decline, and that since the middle of the 1980s a slow increase has resumed, becoming quite marked following Pope Benedict's Motu Proprio *Summorum Pontificum* of July 7, 2007 (with a doubling of the number of traditional Masses worldwide between 2007 and 2017). It is moreover clear that the average age of those attending is less than that in the majority of the parishes (it is in rough terms equivalent to those attending the Masses of the Emmanuel Community[14]).

The bishops did not turn a blind eye to the Tridentine celebrations which took place from 1969 onward (in some cases, for various reasons, they expressly approved them), and so the number of "affairs" multiplied: curés relieved of their posts, priests receiving censures (there were some cases of priests suspended *a divinis*, that is, forbidden to celebrate the sacraments), celebrations accompanied by demonstrations in the sanctuaries, marches on Rome, and disruptions of particularly provocative celebrations of the new rite. The community founded by Monsignor Lefebvre, who had resigned from his post of Superior General of the Fathers of the Holy Spirit on September 30, 1968, became a reservoir of priests who did not accept the new rite. He opened a *convict*, or religious hostel, in Switzerland, at Fribourg, in October 1969, and then a seminary at Écône, in the diocese of Sion, in October of 1970. To this end he obtained the respective authorizations of Monsignor Charrière, Bishop of Fribourg (who, on November 1, 1970, established Lefebvre's foundation as a Pious Union legally recognized by the diocese, under the title of "The International Priestly Fraternity of Saint Pius X," for a period of six months, renewable), and of Monsignor Adam, Bishop of Sion.

---

[14] The Emmanuel Community provides numerous mission churches in France drawing substantial congregations. The age balance of these congregations is similar to that of the congregations of the SSPX.

The growth of the *affaire Lefebvre* (which included a suspension *a divinis* on July 22, 1976, and the excommunications of July 1, 1988) had a certain inevitability about it, to the extent that whether on the one side or on the other discussion of the basic doctrinal issue was avoided (in his Declaration of November 21, 1974, Marcel Lefebvre had written, "It is impossible to modify profoundly the *lex orandi* without modifying the *lex credendi*"[15]) in favor of a purely disciplinary dispute: whether or not "the tradition" was permitted, whether or not ordinations had been authorized. In reality, of course, everyone knew that what was at stake was the Council and that a justification, whether of the "resistance" of the one side or of the sanctions imposed by the other side, could only be reached on a doctrinal basis: "The point of departure [of the celebrations of the Tridentine Mass] is always the non-acceptance of the work of the Second Vatican Council," noted the report of the enquiry demanded by Cardinal Knox, Prefect of the Congregation for the Sacraments and Divine Worship.[16]

Little by little, a network of places where traditional Masses were celebrated extended over France, served either by parish curés or by priests following the Tridentine rite and coming from various foundations. Since then, these foundations have flourished openly, benefiting from the official acts of tolerance accorded to the Priestly Fraternity of Saint Pius X at the Lefebvre-Ratzinger talks, which in 1988 preceded the autonomous ordinations of bishops by Monsignor Lefebvre. The "capture" of the Paris church of Saint-Nicholas-du-Chardonnet by the followers of Monsignor Ducaud-Bourget, a former chaplain of the Order of Malta, in 1977, came to symbolize rejection of the liturgical reform. It is worth noting that

---

[15] "The Declaration of 21 November 1974," http://www.archbishoplefebvre.com/november-21-1974.html (accessed June 22, 2024).

[16] "Il punto di partenza è sempre la non accettazione dell'operato del Concilio Vaticano II," *Notitiae*, 185, vol. 17 (1981), no. 12, 607.

the long-term tenure of Saint-Nicholas-du-Chardonnet by its new occupants was the fruit of arbitration by the government. Cardinal Marty had in reality immediately obtained an order for the expulsion of the occupants, but the Minister of the Interior, Michel Poniatowski, and his successor, Christian Bonnet, advised them that they would refuse to allow the police to be involved, citing the necessity of allowing all religious sensibilities a share in the public space.

Pressure from the traditionalists matched the concerns of Cardinal Ratzinger, Prefect of the Congregation for the Doctrine of the Faith, within whose province in Rome the matter fell. A circular letter, *Quattuor abhinc Annos*, from the Congregation for Divine Worship, dated October 3, 1984, granted diocesan bishops the faculty to make use of an *indult* by which those faithful who requested it could have the benefit of the Mass celebrated according to the Roman missal in the standard edition of 1962.

Then, following Monsignor Lefebvre's ordinations without apostolic mandate of four bishops on June 30, 1988, John Paul II's Motu Proprio *Ecclesia Dei* of July 2, 1988 decreed that priests of the traditional rite could set up institutes dedicated to the traditional liturgy, and created a Pontifical Commission, the Commission *Ecclesia Dei*, on which these institutes would depend, and which was also charged with regulating the authorizations given by diocesan bishops for the use in their dioceses of the Tridentine missal.

On July 7, 2007 came *Summorum Pontificum*. Pressed by a controversy which it was impossible to smother, and which had now reached the highest levels, the pope, in his capacity as supreme legislator for the Church, was forced stage by stage to allow the coexistence of the former state of the Roman rite, now called the "extraordinary form," and the new state, called the "ordinary form." Pope Francis's Motu Proprio *Traditionis Custodes* of July 16, 2021, confirmed by the apostolic letter *Desiderio Desideravi* of June 29, 2022, and a series of texts and decisions, have tried to go back on the arrangements of *Summorum Pontificum*. They have created a confused situation, which shows every sign of being an interim solution: the former *lex orandi* is not about to give up the ghost.

A sociological study of the priests and faithful of the traditional rite has yet to be made. It is possible to suggest that the socio-religious category which was thus created at the end of the 1960s and in the 1970s only partially incorporates the heirs of the integrist Catholicism that was hostile to the *Ralliement*, but that its creation results rather from a sort of reaction provoked by an analogous phenomenon: the feeling that Rome was giving way in the face of modern society. We also need to take account of the fact that the traditionalist liturgical reaction profits from, and even shares in, the very phenomenon to which it is opposed, namely the introduction into the Church of liberalism and the questioning of hierarchical authority. Today, in reality, now that free choice has been absorbed into Catholicism, it is much easier to imagine rejecting the liturgy of Paul VI than it was for a late nineteenth-century Catholic to think of criticizing the political directives of Leo XIII (and *a fortiori* than it was for a Catholic of the 1930s to read *L'Action Française* and run the risk of being denied the sacraments by his parish priest).

Opinion polling in 1976 showed, to the great astonishment of the hierarchy, that the Lefebvrist competition in particular, and traditionalist competition in general, met with a sympathetic response from a large percentage of Catholics. And then they continue to cry out, "We have not explained the Council properly"! Explanations have continued, but the phenomenon remains. The number of regular practicing Catholics is today greatly diminished (in some dioceses there has been an 80 percent reduction in the last thirty years). To different degrees, a good portion of observant Catholics, if we can borrow the language of Yann Raison du Cleuziou, have not ceased their silent opposition to the clergy marked by the post-conciliar militancy.

But even before the reform's principal opponent, Monsignor Lefebvre, was sanctioned by suspension *a divinis*, the reform's principal architect had experienced the ingratitude of those in power. A Roman career such as that of Annibale Bugnini should logically have been crowned with the purple of the cardinalate. His exile in 1975 to a minor ambassadorship (he was nominated as pronuncio to Teheran) showed Paul VI's deep disappointment. It is hardly likely that the pope believed the rumors concerning Bugnini's membership in the Freemasons which circulated in the very heart of the Curia, but he made his over-zealous minister pay for the bitterness of his disillusion.

As for the new Mass which from now on would bear his name, Paul VI had dreamed that men would see it as the radiant demonstration of this period of a conciliar "springtime." It was nothing more than banalities in shades of grey. And above all, within the lifeless body of Catholicism, it had become the sign of the incurable division which Vatican II had introduced.

CONCLUSION

Toward a Reform of the Church

WITH THE PASSAGE of time, we have seen clearly what some people, such as Michel de Certeau, diagnosed already in the 1960s: following Vatican II there has been a rent, one might even say a schism, separating the Church into two currents, each of them composite but easily identifiable. For the first it was necessary at the very least to prevent further development based on the Council, and for the second the Council was merely a starting-point. Even while the Council was in session, the great problem which had to be resolved by Paul VI, who directed the Council from the second session onward, was that of unity: the more the Church splintered into fragments, the more "the ecclesiology of communion" was invoked.

Re-establishing unity on the basis of a Council that did not itself claim to be infallible Magisterium has been the cross on which the post-conciliar popes have suffered. They have failed. The popes of restoration, John Paul II and Benedict XVI, just as much as the pope of progress, Francis, each of the three in his own manner, could not even maintain the fiction of unity. Leo XIV, who is a direct heir of Francis and more generally of Vatican II, will not be able to do any better if he is held fast in the same straitjacket.

Shortly after his election, in his well-known address to the Curia, Benedict XVI distinguished two interpretations of the conciliar reform, the "hermeneutic of discontinuity and rupture," which he considered pernicious, and the "hermeneutic of reform or of renewal in continuity," which he made his own, and which was designed, he said, to prevent "a rupture between the pre-conciliar Church and the post-conciliar Church."[1] In summary, Benedict had defined what in a liberal democracy—whose modes of thinking had come more and more to permeate the Church—would be called a center-right, which he legitimized, and a center-left, which he ruled out.

There was no question for Benedict XVI of joining the traditionalist "rejectionist front," which to differing degrees refused to accept one or both of the Council and its liturgy. For all that, because of the fact of his interest in and support for the pre-conciliar liturgy, Benedict XVI had the opportunity to go further than a hermeneutic of renewal in continuity. His "restorationist" approach could have become the starting-point for a process of transition, like that which took place under John XXIII, but in the opposite direction. The situations were in fact comparable, but in an inverse way, comparable also in the uncertainty over the initial wishes of the popes concerned: John XXIII did not perhaps have the intention of launching the Church on the conciliar adventure in the way in which matters eventually turned out, but he had taken actions, taken risks, and made nominations, which in reality first destabilized the antimodern world-view (the product of the Tridentine world-view, itself begotten by the Gregorian world-view, and in place until the time of Pius XII), and then brought the Church out of it. In a similar situation, but the other way around, Benedict XVI, who was not anti-conciliar, could nevertheless, following the line of *Summorum Pontificum*, have taken actions, made nominations, taken risks, and particularly liturgical risks, which could have destabilized the conciliar edifice.

---

[1] Benedict XVI, *Address to the Roman Curia*, December 22, 2005. A hermeneutic is a method or style of interpretation. Pope Benedict argued that under the "hermeneutic of discontinuity and rupture" the documents of Vatican II were presumed to break with the previous teaching of the Church, and that under the "hermeneutic of reform in continuity" those same documents were presumed to be in continuity with that teaching.

Nevertheless, as we all know, the process—including everything related to renewal in continuity—came to a halt midstream: not only did the Church not see its way to rejecting the Council, but restorationism,[2] the halting of any further movement by the conciliar movement, was seen as a failure, an experiment that had not borne fruit. The Church in the West continued to vanish from the public space, the numbers of its clerical personnel—priests, religious, seminarians—continued to shrink, and the center in Rome seemed no longer to be governed. Benedict XVI, who had become the target of those adhering to the "hermeneutic of discontinuity," retreated into his theologian's study, anticipating in effect the resignation on which he finally resolved in 2013.

Entirely naturally (as it seemed, but in fact as the result of much preliminary canvassing), the 2013 conclave tried the alternative option, that of the center-left, the "hermeneutic" of a Vatican II under attack, which Jorge Bergoglio had espoused. The new pope, who in 2022 said that he was engaged in a struggle against "restorationism," which wanted to "muzzle" the Council, and against "traditionalism," which wanted to strip the Council of significance, devoted himself to, as he himself put it, "pulling down walls."[3]

The "walls" included those of *Humanae Vitae* and the whole set of texts that followed this encyclical, which had preserved conjugal morality from the liberalization which Vatican II had imposed on ecclesiology. *Amoris*

---

[2] Restorationism is the belief that at some point in the past things were correctly managed, and that the solution to today's difficulties is at the least (as here) to halt further movement away from the point when things were correctly managed, or more positively, actually to work towards the restoration of the previous position. In the liturgical context, restorationists believe that the liturgy reached a state of near perfection at some point in the past, and that the solution to the Church's liturgical problems is to restore the previous state of the liturgy.

[3] In conversation with the editors of European Jesuit journals on May 19, 2022, reported by *La Civiltà Cattolica*, June 14, 2022.

Laetitia declared in 2016 that persons living publicly in an adulterous relationship could continue to do so without incurring grave sin.[4]

The "walls" also included those of *Summorum Pontificum*, which had granted legal recognition to the academy of the pre-conciliar Church formed by the historic liturgy with its teaching and its clerical personnel. *Traditionis Custodes* and *Desiderio Desideravi* cancelled this attempt at "return": the new liturgical books, said the former, "are the unique expression of the *lex orandi* of the Roman rite."[5]

But the Bergoglio option failed as had the Ratzinger option previously: the ecclesial institution has continued to founder and its sense of mission has continued to disappear. And just as disillusion crystallized around the absence of governance under Benedict XVI, so under Francis criticisms of the excesses of a muddled and dictatorial governance (despite the catchword of synodality) became more and more obvious. Moreover, just as Benedict XVI never took the risk of reversing the developments since the Council, so Francis took great care not to risk setting off an institutional explosion by going beyond the Council: for example, despite all his denunciations of clericalism, he did not really challenge clerical celibacy, nor did he open the priesthood to women.[6]

That, very precisely, was the mandate that Leo XIV was given by his electors at the conclave of May 2025: continue with the policy of the Bergoglian interpretation of the Council, while doing everything possible to bring peace to a Church in torment. Is that possible? Can the Church be united on any other basis than that of the unity of the faith?

---

[4] Francis, Apostolic Exhortation *Amoris Laetitia*, March 19, 2016, no. 301.

[5] Francis, Motu Proprio *Traditionis Custodes*, July 16, 2021, art. 1.

[6] Clericalism is the belief that priests should be paid a particular respect or should be conceded special political power. The word is nearly always used derogatively, as here, to mean paying an exaggerated respect to priests or giving them undeserved power or status.

Thus, neither the attempt to present a more moderate version of the Council, nor the attempt to maximize it, has halted the flow of blood, which has continued ineluctably. What is more, the split has widened, in the sense that the conservative end of the axis, that of observant Catholics, has grown stronger. To begin with, relatively stronger, since it has suffered fewer losses than the progressive end, which is failing to renew itself. And also because, during the pontificate of Francis, there was a strengthening of the alliance between the adherents of the "hermeneutic of reform in continuity," the restorationists, and the "rejection front," traditionalism, which was more in evidence than ever.

So, what can happen next? The gentle medicine which Leo XIV seems to want to administer to a patient in a terminal state can at best only prolong the suffering. Inevitably, we will need to proceed to a doctrinal and spiritual recentering, accompanied by a recognition of the break that has taken place. In the shorter or longer term, as always in the Church, which is *semper reformanda*, that can only happen in the form of a return to the Church's evangelical roots. It will be necessary, reversing the famous formula of *The Leopard*, for nothing to change (in doctrine and in morality) in order for everything to change (for the entirety of the Church's daily life to change).[7] That will require reformers, holy and strong prelates, with a project that is theological, and thus magisterial and spiritual and of all-embracing extent, guided by the provident hand of God.

But before then, in the short to medium term—under Leo XIV? in the outer reaches of his administration?—we can visualize a period of transition in which an ecclesiastic of the highest rank, formed in the conciliar mold but not wishing to see Catholicism perish will, despite himself, or perhaps of his own accord, concede full liberty to all

---

[7] Giuseppe di Lampedusa, *Il Gattopardo* (*The Leopard*) (Milan: Feltrinelli, 1958).

the vital forces which produce fruit in the form of the transmission from one generation to another, of the faith, of vocations, and of mission. In that way, in accordance with the promises made by Christ, there will gradually emerge a true reform of the Church.

INDEX

ABBÉ CLAUDE BARTHE (b. 1947) is the author of numerous works on the current crisis of the Church and of articles in various journals commenting on religious affairs. He has devoted particular attention to defending and elucidating the "genius" of the traditional Roman liturgy.

www.ingramcontent.com/pod-product-compliance
Lightning Source LLC
LaVergne TN
LVHW090607110826
845146LV00001B/293

* 9 7 9 8 8 9 2 8 0 1 7 7 5 *